The whole BIBLE in a year FOR CHILDREN

50 LESSONS
FROM GENESIS TO REVELATION!

The whole BIBLE in a year

FOR CHILDREN

50 LESSONS
FROM GENESIS TO REVELATION!

e625.com

HOWARD ANDRUEJOL   WILLY GÓMEZ

e625.com

The whole Bible in a year: Lessons for children
Howard Andruejol, Willy Gómez
Originally published in Spanish
Published by e625® © 2024
Dallas, Texas Estados Unidos de América.

ISBN: 978-1-9541495-0-2

Translated by: David Ortíz
Disgned by: Creatorstudio.net

TABLE OF CONTENTS

"All Scripture is inspired by God and is profitable".

2nd Timothy 3:16 (CSB)

We are very happy to bring you this series of lessons from the whole Bible. Studying this series will take you on a fascinating tour of a library that consists of sixty six volumes, which allows you to get to know God's character, his perfect work, and his wonderful expectations towards us.

Today, many churches have developed the harmful habit of reading the biblical texts in small fragments. If you pay attention, you'll notice how in classes, small groups, preaching, devotionals, and daily reading planners, it has become common practice to read isolated portions of the Bible. This is not necessarily wrong, but if we develop the habit of reading it only in this manner, we run the risk of taking the loose texts as snacks, or even as if they were phrases of the horoscope. On the other hand, to delve deeper into the complete story and take the time to notice its details and its application, helps us to ensure that later on we will have a better understanding of those loose texts.

Try this exercise: Ask 10 Christians, of any age, something as simple As "What is the Bible about?", and you will get 12 different answers. Ask them to explain to you how the Old and New Testaments relate, and possibly some will begin to hesitate. If you want to go a bit further, ask them to explain to you what the book of Obadiah is about, and how it relates to the rest of the Bible and to us today.

These should not be questions that only seminarians or pastors are able to answer. All believer s need to be able to understand them, and that is why this material is so important.

The reason for this is very simple. Imagine for a moment a jigsaw puzzle, one that's difficult to put together. Would it have a thousand pieces? A thousand five hundred? Let's imagine one that has two thousand pieces, and let's try the following experiment. Imagine now that I take the puzzle box, and hide the cover that contains the image that must be put together. Then I will ask you to put in your hand randomly, and take out only ten pieces. Now comes the interesting part; What if I asked you to describe the image? Do you think you'd be able to do it? Of course not! You could make something up, but you certainly would not be able to guess the image as such.

At many churches throughout the continent we asked the same question. What are the most famous biblical texts that all churches know? At every city where we tried this exercise, the response was always the same ten verses.
Yes, just ten verses. It appears that our new generations are growing up with only 10 of the 31,130 pieces of the biblical puzzle. And with those ten verses, we expect them to have a clear picture of God's character, his perfect work, and his expectation towards us. It's an impossible request. They will undoubtedly develop an image that's false, incomplete, distorted and disfigured.

Just as it is important to appreciate the fine detail of each piece of the puzzle, it is also indispensable to be able to see the complete picture. And that's what these lessons are about.

We have prepared this manual as much as possible as a chronological journey through God's revelation, from Genesis to Revelation. It is our hope that, having an overview of the biblical books, your students will react in two ways.

First, that they'll be able to say, "now I understand what this book is about!" Each lesson will be effective to the extent that each participant is able to have a better understanding of the content and purpose of the books of the Bible.

As you will see, since this adventure is designed for a full year of lessons, it is not possible to include all 66 books in 50 of them. It has been a difficult decision to compress, summarize or omit. Moreover, we are convinced that Genesis on its own should take us through 50 weeks! We are confident that we are building a solid foundation, and that we will continue to build on it, with more in-depth studies of the specific books. We are looking forward to what will follow from this.

Second, that by understanding better the full picture, they will now be motivated to learn more about the details. If they are able to connect each book of the Bible to the complete image of the puzzle, it will make it easier for each individual chapter to make sense. We want to develop devout readers of the biblical text, scholars of God's word. Join them on this tour, help them to explore the richness of each individual biblical passage. Take the time to develop new series about specific books of the Bible, as well as complete biographies of biblical characters.

In addition to considering the maturity and contextual characteristics of each age group, we have chosen to approach these series through a lens with which to look at the biblical books. With it we underline the great theological and anthropological themes of the Bible.

Each volume is unique, and complementary. Those who travel with us through these four books will certainly have a clear idea of what the Bible is about!

The children's volume was developed around an identity that's outside of this world. The biblical journey will focus on the progressive revelation of God's character. Who is He? How does He present Himself to humans? Knowing God allows us also know our own identity: What is our natural condition? How is this identity manifested in our behavior? We need to be rescued from this condition, with Jesus Christ being our only hope. To receive him as Lord and Savior renews us. Who are we now in Christ? How does this transformation manifest itself in our behavior?

The volume for pre-adolescents focuses on an unconditional and eternal relationship. The biblical journey will focus on God's initiative to relate to humans. It will highlight the invincible obstacle for man - sin, and Christ's complete victory. The emphasis is on God's faithfulness to man - despite our infidelity - and the closeness that it allows us, only through Christ. What defines God's relationship with us? What should I do to live that relationship today?

The volume for teenagers focuses on crucial decisions. The biblical journey will focus on God's expectations, given our new identity, of lives lived according to his character. We will study the divine perspective in order to make the right decisions in every facet of our lives, the purpose of holiness, and the dire consequences of disobedience. The gospel is not focused on our behavior, but given the Grace of God, our best response is to glorify Him.

The volume for university students is missionary. The biblical journey will focus on God's mission, which seeks to redeem the human being. Special attention will be paid to how God has has at all times and will continue to fulfill until the end his plan for human beings. Salvation is available to anyone. Our new identity sends us to explain this gospel to every person, even to the most remote places on the planet. This is our true life purpose, to live in mission here and there, now.

On our website, www.e625.com, you will find supplementary material for our lessons. Our goal for the conversations that arise in each lesson is that they be theologically deep and didactically creative.

Of course, all this has been the work of a great team of people involved in the design of the curriculum and instruction. Upon hearing the idea, many friends enthusiastically joined this project. To each of you, THANK YOU for investing in the Biblical formation of our new generations!

Let's lead them to know the whole puzzle, to have a biblical image of the person of God, to understand His eternal plan, and the response He expects from each one of us.

Let us learn together!

Howard Andruejol y Lucas Leys
General editors.

HOW TO USE THIS BOOK

The Bible is a collection of sixty-six books inspired by God. For those of us who believe in God, the Bible contains God's thoughts for our lives.

The Bible is our guide, and the source of wisdom for our lives. We must:

- Believe it
- Honor it
- Love it
- Obey it
- Keep it in our heart
- Preach it
- Study it

The structure of this book

This book was designed with the thought of helping the church and parents become a team in order to teach our children the Word of God. It is an exciting and entertaining tour through each of the books of the Bible.

The essential element of this material is the question. There are more than three hundred questions designed to generate meaningful conversations with our children. This will enable us to help them understand that the Bible is a conversation between God and us.

Each lesson has the following structure:

NAME OF THE BOOK

General information about the book

The general concept of the book and the number of chapters it contains.

Who wrote it and in what era?

Information about the author of the book, and a simple description of the time when it was written.

Purpose of the book

The reason why this book was put in the Bible.

Introductory activity
Description of an introductory activity. Usually it's a game, used to engage our apprentices in the history and introduce the discussion. The game must be as challenging as possible. We give a suggestion for a game, but you can propose your own ideas.

Remember that starting with a game stimulates learning, connects us with our audience and generates knowledge prior to the discussion.

 **Let's connect**: A small recommendation about what to say when finishing the game, to enable us to connect it to the story. It is not intended to be a complete talk, but rather a few brief words to connect with the discussion.

Initial discussion:
   • A question that is given to the small group, so that the majority of the group members can speak. This space is designed to a.low them to express themselves. We should not interrupt them, but listen to them and generate an environment of trust, so that subsequent conversations may be deeper.

What do we learn about God in this book?:

A recommendation for a biblical reading, and its explanation or application.

 Question for us: To ask of each group member. We emphasize the need for each boy and girl to talk.

Knowing God better: Closing the discussion to explain the point of the reading.

A CHARACTERISTIC OF GOD'S CHARACTER

 Main characters:
The outstanding characters from this book.

 Recommendation of verse to memorize:
Recommend a verse to memorize during the week.

What other verses would you add?

_____   _____
_____   _____
_____   _____

Download the "Family Readings and Conversations" from: www.e625.com/lessons

Recommended daily readings with a related question to enable parents to generate a discussion after the reading. This section is designed for parents and children to do once daily. Download these documents from our website, **www.e625.com**.

To get more out of the teaching-learning time, consider these guiding ideas:

• **The questions are as important as the answers.** This book is designed to study the Bible on weekends at church or together as a family, based on the question as the didactic element.

• **We do not use crayons and worksheets.** We do not want the study of the Bible to be thought of as yet one more school class. We set out to design activities where resources such as crayons or worksheets are not used, to force us to think of more energizing and creative activities.

• **Let's avoid as much as we can the master class.** People learn best through discussion and activity. We design this material to minimize the use of master exposition. This will allow more people to collaborate in teaching the Bible to our children.

• **Small groups.** We recommend carrying out the Bible study in small groups, between eight and twelve children per group. This will allow for more discussion.

• **Many people doing few things.** We believe that it will be best if we get more dads involved in the team of teaching children the Bible. This material is designed to simplify this process and involve more people in teaching.

OLD TESTAMENT

The whole
BIBLE
in a year
→ FOR ←
CHILDREN

Lesson 1 > GENESIS (Part one)

Chapters 1 to 10:
General information about the Book
The book of Genesis is called the "book of origins". It is part of the Pentateuch. It has 50 chapters.

Who wrote it, and in what era?
The author of the book of Genesis has not been identified, and is believed to have been Moses. The narration of the work of God begins in the eternal past, and it describes creation until it arrives at man and the first heroes of the faith.

Purpose of the book
This book introduces us to the Pentateuch (which are the first five books of the Bible) and for a long time it was the scripture available to God's people. It explains to us why man needs to be saved due to sin. The outcome of this book is goes all the way to Revelation (the last book of the Bible).

Introductory activity
Load the Ship
Let's make a little boat with a blank sheet of paper, and put it in a bowl with water. Let's add weight to the paper boat and shake the water with a small stick, to see how much our boat can stand.

Let's connect: Creating things is a process. Today we will learn about the first part of the book of Genesis, which shows God as creator, until we reach the story of Noah and the flood.

Initial discussion:
• How long did it take you to make the boat? To create things takes time, and it's a process. We will see how God created the heavens, the earth and all that's in it, taking some time and leading a process.

? What do we learn about God in this book?

(Genesis 1:1-31)

In Genesis we are told how the heavens and the earth, plants, animals, man and woman were created. Creation occurs in seven days, and God rested on the seventh day. When God created humans, He realized that he had created something very good.

 Question for us: What was the most difficult job you ever did (create a video, put together a toy, some homework from school)? How did you feel when you finished it?

 Knowing God better: It took God seven days to CREATE the world, but when He finished, He felt very satisfied with what he had done. We know that God is our creator and gave us the great gift of CREATIVITY, to enable us to do stuff. Every time you create something, remember your God Creator.

GOD IS CREATOR

(Genesis 2, 3 and 4)

Genesis also presents God wanting to relate to humans and shows us how, despite our mistakes, He remains close to us. In this section, humanity's sin appears, when Adam and Eve disobey, influenced by the snake, by eating the forbidden fruit; Then they realize that they have sinned, and seek to hide from God. They are expelled from the garden as a sign that our disobedience has consequences, but God never stops caring for them.

When Adam and Eve leave Eden they have children. The first were Cain and Abel. They also worshiped God but Cain got angry because God preferred the offering presented by Abel, and decided to kill him! Amazing! God decides to punish Cain as a result of his actions.

 Question for us: Can you remember an occasion in which your disobedience brought you negative consequences?

 Knowing God better: Even when we make mistakes, God can forgive us if we seek Him, but sometimes he allows us to have consequences so we can learn from our mistakes. He does it because he loves us and because He is our Father. Our parents correct us because they love us.

GOD IS FAIR.
GOD IS LOVING.

(Genesis 6 and 7)

Genesis goes on to tell us that evil spread on earth; few people remembered God. They did whatever they wanted: they stole from others and ruined the world that God had created. God saw that the world had become evil and decided to sweep away everything and start over.

He noticed Noah, who did seek God. Noah had a wife and three children: Shem, Ham and Japheth. God asked Noah to build an ark because he was going to flood the world for forty days. (It had never rained before). Noah, facing the mockery of everyone else, decided to heed God. When the rain came, only Noah and his family, along with a couple of each species of animals, were saved. They were saved because they obeyed God, despite the mockery of everyone else.

 Question for us: Can you remember an occasion in which you have done what's right before God even though others did not understand you or made fun of you?

 Knowing God better: Sometimes doing the right thing is not the most popular option, but in the end we can see that doing the right thing is always the best option. The result is not always Immediate, and sometimes we have to wait some time to see the benefit of doing what's right. For example, when you study for an exam sometimes you don't see the immediate benefits, because you have to stop playing, but when you see your good grade you realize that doing the right thing was worth it.

GOD IS PATIENT.

 Main characters:
Adam and Eve: the first humans.
Cain and Abel: children of Adam and Eve.
Noah: man who sought God and built the ark.

 Recommendation of verse to memorize:
Genesis 1:1
In the beginning God created the heavens and the earth.

What other verses would you add?

——————   ———————————————————————————
——————   ———————————————————————————
——————   ———————————————————————————

 Download the "Family Readings and Conversations" from:
www.e625.com/lessons

Lesson 2 > GENESIS (Part two)

Chapters 11 to 50:

General information about the Book
The book of Genesis is called the "book of origins".
It is part of the Pentateuch.
It has 50 chapters.

Who wrote it, and in what era?
The author of the book of Genesis has not been identified, and is believed to have been Moses. The narration of the work of God begins in the eternal past, and it describes creation until it arrives at man and the first heroes of the faith.

Purpose of the book
The second part of this book (Chapters 11 to 50) helps us see the effects of a strong faith in God, and tells us the story of his people.

Introductory activity
Adam is the father of Cain, Abel and Seth. Set is the father of Noah. Noah is the father of Shem, Ham and Japheth. Shem is Terah's father. Terah is the father of Haran and Abraham. Abraham is the father of Ishmael, Isaac and Midian. Isaac is the father of Jacob and Esau. Jacob is the father of Joseph (the dreamer) and his eleven brothers. With this information, let's answer the following questions:

- Who is Joseph's great grandfather?
- What are the names of Noah's great-great grandchildren?
- What are the names of Noah's uncles?

Let's connect: God takes care of our generations. The Bible teaches us that if we believe in the Lord Jesus Christ, we and our family will be saved. In Genesis we see that God is known as the God of Abraham, Isaac and Jacob.

Initial discussion:
• Who in our family believes in God?

What do we learn about God in this book?:

(Genesis 12:1-22:19)

God told Abram to leave his homeland and his relatives, and go to a land that He was going to show him (he did not know where he would go). God promised him that if he did, He would bless him. He listened to God and moved. God Blessed him a lot, and he had to divide the land with his nephew Lot.

Abram always believed God, who had told him that his offspring would be very large, like the stars of the sky or the sand of the sea. The problem was that he was already old and had no children. But he kept believing that nothing is impossible for God. The elderly can no longer have babies, and yet Isaac was born when Abram and his wife Sara were very old. Imagine how happy they were! Then, God told him to offer his son Isaac as a sacrifice (how terrible!). Abram loved his son very much, but he loved God more and decided to obey. When he was about to sacrifice his son, God told him to stop. God was testing Abram's obedience, and he changed Abram's name, by adding an H. That's why we know him as Abraham.

Question for us: When God gives you a gift that you were eagerly expecting, do you prefer the gift over obeying your parents?

Knowing God better: We must not get so attached to the gifts that God gives us, so that we forget to obey our parents or to do the right thing. For example, if a video game that you were expecting causes you to start behaving badly with your parents, it might be best to take that gift away.

GOD IS POWERFUL.

(Genesis 22 to 35)

God remained faithful to Isaac, as he was with his father Abraham. His dad helped him find his wife, Rebecca. God always took care of Isaac. in fact, he opened water wells (which were very difficult to find during that time) and although people unfairly took them away, instead of fighting, Isaac moved on, and God allowed him to find new wells. He gave us a great lesson about trusting God and not clinging to what God gives us.

Isaac had twin sons: Esau and Jacob. Esau decided to sell his rights as the firstborn (which were many at the time) to Jacob in exchange for a plate of lentils. I think he did not value what he had. God's blessing was with Jacob in everything. Even when he chose his wife, his father-in-law wanted to cheat him by giving him bad cattle as a condition to letting him marry his daughter. He put a lot of obstacles on him, like giving him spotted sheep, but in spite of all the obstacles, God blessed him in everything he did, and everything went well for him: he was allowed to marry the wife he wanted.

 Question for us: Do you believe God can take care of us even though there are people who want to harm us?

 Knowing God better: We see in the life of Isaac and Jacob that God is the one who always takes care of us, even though there are people who want to harm us.

GOD IS A CAREGIVER.

(Genesis 35 to 50)

Jacob had twelve children, who represent the twelve tribes of Israel: Reuben, Simon, Levi, Judah, Dan, Naphtali, Asher, Gad, Issachar, Zebulun, Joseph and Benjamin. Among them, Joseph had special treatment because he and Benjamin were children of Rachel, Jacob's second wife. His brothers did not like how Joseph was their father's favorite, and planned to kill him. To make matters worse, Joseph had many dreams and told his brothers dreams in which the moon and the stars bowed before him.

Instead of killing him, they threw him into a hole and sold him as a slave. He was taken to Egypt, where God helped him thrive, and he became the administrator of an important man named Potiphar. Potiphar's wife wanted Joseph for herself, but Joseph knew it was wrong and fled. Then he was unjustly accused and sent to jail (what a terrible and unfair situation for Joseph!). Instead of complaining about his situation, in prison he was blessed by God and became the head of the prisoners. There he met the king's cupbearer and the king's baker.

The king had a dream that only Joseph could interpret. The King placed him as second in command after him. Joseph played an important role in managing the government. Meanwhile, his brothers arrived in Egypt to look for food; they did not know that Joseph lived, much less that he was the one who ran the government. Joseph, instead of taking revenge on his brothers, decided to forgive them, and told them that God had turned the evil they had wanted to do to him into good.

Question for us: Have you experienced a situation in which you needed to forgive someone who hurt you?

 Knowing God better: God takes care of us even when others want to harm us, and the best we can do is decide to forgive. Sometimes it is necessary put some distance for a while, but that should not allow bitterness to stay in our hearts.

GOD IS FORGIVING.

 Main characters:
Abraham: father of our faith.
Isaac: son of Abraham and father of Jacob and Esau.
Jacob: father of the twelve tribes of Israel.
Joseph: the dreamer, son of Jacob.

 Recommendation of verse to memorize:
Genesis 45:5b
It was to save lives that God sent me ahead of you.

What other verses would you add?
————————   —————————————————————————————————
————————   —————————————————————————————————
————————   —————————————————————————————————

 Download the "Family Readings and Conversations" from:
www.e625.com/lessons

Lesson 3 > EXODUS

General information about the book
It is called "the great escape."
It is part of the Pentateuch.
It has 40 chapters.

Who wrote it and in what era?
Like Genesis, it is believed that the writer of this book was Moses. It was written at a time when the Egyptian Empire was large, ruled by Pharaohs who were the highest authority. It was written approximately in the 1500s and 1400s BC.

Purpose of the book
The book is a continuation of Genesis and narrates Israel's liberation from their captivity in Egypt, showing how God takes care of His people in a supernatural way. The people of Israel are sent to the desert, where they learn to know God more closely.

Introductory activity
In the room or in an outdoor area we will mark a starting point and an ending point, well separated from each other. The game consists of trying to get from the starting point to the ending point while others try to prevent it. If they touch us, we must return to the starting point and try again. The difficulty is that we can only move with our legs together, that is, jumping or walking very slowly. One group will try to advance and another group will try to stop them.

Let's connect: Do you realize how difficult it is to get from one point to another when there are people trying to prevent it? That's how Pharaoh wanted to prevent the people of Israel from leaving Egypt. To make matters worse, they ran into the Red Sea.

Initial discussion:
• What do you think the people of Israel were thinking when they ran into the Red Sea, while fleeing and being chased by the Egyptians? What would you have done instead?

What do we learn about God in this book?:

(Exodus 1:1 to 12:36)

Exodus tells how the people of Israel suffered as slaves of the Egyptian people. The Egyptians did not want the Israelites to be liberated so they ordered the killing of all the Israelite boys. Moses' mother hid him and left him in the river inside a basket, begging God to rescue him. Coincidentally, Pharaoh's daughter rescued him and raised him as his son.

When Moses grew up it bothered him how badly they treated the Israelites, to the point that he argued very strongly with someone who was mistreating one and killed him. He had to run away, but then God told him that he had to free his people. Moses didn't want to go because he didn't feel prepared, he was afraid and said that he wasn't a good speaker. He made many excuses not to go, but God told him: "I made you and I know everything about you." He promised to help him in everything, so in the end Moses accepted the challenge.

Pharaoh did not want to free Israel but God sent ten plagues to persuade him to let them go. God told Moses that he was going to give them one last warning. The last of the plagues was the hardest because the eldest children of all the Egyptians died, including Pharaoh's son. In the end, Pharaoh let them go.

Question for us: Have you ever felt unable or incapable of doing an activity you wanted to do?

Knowing God better: God is our deliverer. Many times He wants to free us from our fears and from the things that make us think we can't. God helps us despite our limitations and shows us His power in them.

GOD IS LIBERATOR.
GOD IS ALMIGHTY.
GOD IS OUR TRUST.

(Exodus 14:15 to 15:21)

After letting them go, Pharaoh repented, because he had lost his slaves. He pursued them with horses and troops; about six hundred of his best chariots.

The Israelites, seeing that the Egyptians were chasing them, became very frightened and complained to Moses. They said: "Have you brought us to die in the desert?" Moses was not afraid because a column of fire covered them at night and a cloud guided them by day. When Moses reached the seashore, and there was no escape, God told him to use what he had in his hand (a rod) and lift it. When Moses did, the sea in front of him opened. The Israelites passed and when the Egyptians followed them, the sea closed again and crushed them. God saved the Israelites.

Question for us: Have you been in situations where you thought there was no way out?

Knowing God better: In life we will face many situations in which there seems to be no way out. That is the time to trust God and do our part. God will do what we cannot do.

GOD IS MIRACULOUS.
GOD IS OUR RESCUER.

(Exodus 20)

God wanted to give new rules to the people of Israel, who had grown up as slaves in Egypt. Now they needed help to be able to establish their own Law and to take away what they had learned in slavery. Moses went up a mountain to seek God, and the Lord gave him laws for them to obey. The laws were written in large stones. The laws were:

1. I am the Lord your God. I took you out of Egypt, the country where you were a slave. Do not have any other gods besides me.
2. Do not make any idols.
3. Do not use the name of the Lord your God in vain.
4. The seventh day will be a day of rest to honor the Lord your God.
5. Honor your father and mother, so you can enjoy a long life in the land that the Lord your God gives you.
6. Do not kill.
7. Do not commit adultery.

8. Do not steal.
9. Do not give false testimony against your neighbor.
10. Do not covet your neighbor's house.

He not only gave them commandments but told them how He wanted them to worship Him. He wanted them to build a special tent: a tabernacle. He gave them detailed instructions on the utensils and what it should contain.
The people of Israel had a hard time obeying God and were constantly murmuring and remembering their life in Egypt.

 Question for us: Which of the ten commandments is the hardest for you to obey?

 Knowing God better: God made the commandments not for his benefit but for ours. Living these commandments allows us to live a good life. For example, lying hurts us because in order to cover the lie we have to lie more and the end result ends up being a disaster.

GOD IS GOOD.
GOD IS HOLY.

 Main characters:
Moses: the liberator of Israel from slavery.
Aaron: brother of Moses.
Pharaoh: the oppressor of the Israelites.
Joshua: Moses' assistant.

 Recommendation of verse to memorize:
Exodus 20:12

Honor your father and your mother, so that you may live long in the land the LORD your God is giving you.

What other verses would you add?

_____   _____
_____   _____
_____   _____

 Download the "Family Readings and Conversations" from:
www.e625.com/lessons

Lesson 4 > LEVITUCUS, NUMBERS AND DEUTERONOMY

General information about the book
The name of the book of Leviticus comes from the word Leutikon, which means "Levites subject".
Numbers describes the history of Israel during almost thirty-nine years of circling in the desert.
Deuteronomy explains the law of Moses.
They are part of the Pentateuch.
Leviticus has 27 chapters, Numbers 36 and Deuteronomy 34.

Who wrote it and in what era?
These books, like the others in the Pentateuch, are believed to have been written by Moses in the year 1445 BC.

Purpose of the book
The book of Leviticus was written to instruct the priests on how to lead the people in worship of God. In addition, its goal is to instruct the people in how to lead a holy life.
Numbers tells the story of the people of Israel and their journey through the desert, while Deuteronomy is left to explain more deeply the law of Moses to a new generation.

Introductory activity
Let's play hide and seek. Count to twenty, and someone is going to hide a bunch of grapes (real, plastic or drawn). All of us who are present will look for this bunch of grapes until we find it. Let's observe the attitude each of us has during the game.

Let's connect: Moses sent some spies to see what the promised land was like. Some came with an attitude of fear after seeing giants and many problems. But two of the spies came with an attitude of hope and with a large bunch of grapes and other fruits.

Initial discussion:
• When you have a significant challenge, do you think more about the problems you will face or about the benefits you will receive?

What do we learn about God in these books?

(Leviticus 1:1 to 7:38)

The book of Leviticus explains how the Israelites could present offerings to be accepted by God, and live a life in holiness. Jesus came to present himself as the greatest offering to God, so that we can have a direct relationship with our Father. The Israelites had various types of offerings, each with a specific purpose and meaning for their lives.

The offerings were for forgiveness of sins, for gratitude, for peace, etc. God did not want to focus on the offerings themselves, but on the attitude with which they were presented.

 Question for us: How can we show our gratitude to God today?

 Knowing God better: Jesus is the great offering for our sins and for our peace. God is not interested in our sacrifices or offerings if they are not made with the right attitude. What God sees is our heart. Jesus saw a woman who gave just two cents, and said that she had given more than the rich who had given large amounts of money in the offering. That is because the woman who gave the two cents gave them with a better attitude than the others. She gave everything she had. God wants us to offer our hearts with a good attitude.

GOD IS HOLY.

(Numbers 22:21-31)

God always takes care of his people. There was a king named Balaam, whom God listened to. Some of the kings who were on the road through which the people of Israel were traveling got frightened and went to speak to Balaam, asking him to curse the Israelites. Balaam did not know much about them, and decided to ask God. God told him not to curse them, and added that He would tell him what to do.

Balaam grabbed a donkey and embarked on his journey (without asking God what he wanted). God sent an angel to warn him and to tell him what to do. As Balaam did not stop to ask God, the angel made the donkey speak so that Balaam would stop. In fact, the angel told him that if the donkey had not spoken to him and stopped him, Balaam would have died from his sword. Sometimes God uses even donkeys to talk to us.

Question for us: Do we ask God what he wants us to do before starting a day, or do we just go out without asking Him?

Knowing God better: If we seek God's direction about what we should do, God will speak to us in one way or another. We must be attentive to listen to God because he can speak to us in different ways. Sometimes he will speak through something that stops us, sometimes through our parents, sometimes through his Word, or sometimes through a donkey.

GOD IS PATIENT.
GOD SPEAKS TO US.

(Deuteronomy 30:19-20)

Before he died, Moses wanted to make it clear to the people of Israel that they should seek God and be generous with each other. We always have the choice between doing good and doing evil, between the blessing and the curse. It is up to us to choose wisely. Moses said to them: "This day I call the heavens and the earth as witnesses against you that I have set before you life and death, blessings and curses. Now choose life, so that you and your children may live, and that you may love the Lord your God, listen to his voice, and hold fast to him. For the Lord is your life, and he will give you many years in the land he swore to give to your fathers, Abraham, Isaac and Jacob".

Question for us: What will you choose? The blessing or the curse?

Knowing God better: Every day we have to make decisions between good and evil. We must know God better through his Word to learn more about how to do good and how to choose God's blessing.

GOD IS HE WHO BLESSES ME.

Main characters:
Moses: the leader who spoke with God.
Joshua: the assistant to whom Moses left the leadership.
Aaron: the brother of Moses.
Balaam: He obeyed God, although reluctantly.

Recommendation of verse to memorize:
Deuteronomy 6:4-5

Hear, O Israel: The Lord our God, the Lord is one. Love the Lord your God with all your heart and with all your soul and with all your strength.

What other verses would you add?

_____   _____
_____   _____
_____   _____

Download the "Family Readings and Conversations" from: www.e625.com/lessons

Lesson 5 > JOSHUA

General information about the book
Brave warrior of God.
The book chronicles the conquest of Canaan.
It has 24 chapters.

Who wrote it and in what era?
Most likely the writer was Joshua. Some say that one of his assistants finished it. It may have been written between 1405 and 1385 B.C.

Purpose of the book
It is the first of the historical books. It narrates the exploits of Joshua as he leads in the conquest of the promised land. Joshua means "The Lord is salvation."

Introductory activity
With several sheets of paper we will build the tallest wall we can. Let's build it creatively. We have a time limit of five minutes. At the end, we try to tear it down just by shouting.

Let's connect: God sent Joshua to go around the walls of Jericho seven times, and to tear them down with praise and shouts.

Initial discussion:
• This is an example of how the power of praise can tear down walls and barriers. How wonderful it feels to shout freely! :)

What do we learn about God in this book?:

(Joshua 5:13)
Joshua prepared to conquer Jericho. He sent some spies, and a woman named Rahab helped them by hiding them, and then by giving them a way to escape after they were discovered. She only asked them to save her when they invaded the city. It is interesting that this woman appears in Jesus' family tree.

The Lord told Joshua to camp outside Jericho and to walk around the city for six days. On the seventh day they were to march seven times around the city playing their trumpets and when the trumpet played a long note, Joshua was to order the people to shout, and then the city walls would fall. As crazy as the order seemed, Joshua obeyed, and the walls fell.

Question for us: With what attitude do you think they shouted? Do you think they do it with strength and with lots of joy, or without desire and angry? With what attitude do you sing to God?

 Knowing God better: Often we do not understand the power of praising God. Sometimes, it doesn't seem to make much sense to sing to someone we don't see, but if you think about it, our praise is similar to the shouts at Jericho. What worked about that strategy was not the strength of the shouts, but the obedience in doing it.

GOD IS CREATIVE.
GOD IS STRATEGIC.

(Joshua 7)

After they were victorious in Jericho, Joshua thought that all the other cities would be easier to conquer, and he ran into a city called Hai. The city was small so they thought it would be easy to conquer. The problem was that God had told them not to take anything from the city, and a soldier named Achan disobeyed. So, although it looked easy, they were defeated. Joshua retired to ask God why they had been defeated, and God showed him Achan's sin. After Joshua dealt with it, they won the victory, and continued to conquer thirty-two more kingdoms. Joshua's people were victorious conquerers.

 Question for us: What happens when we trust in ourselves too much and think something will be very easy? Have you ever had an unpleasant surprise for trusting too much in yourself?

 Knowing God better: As simple as a task may look, we must always put our trust in God. The Bible says that God is near the humble and far from the proud. Always keep an attitude of humility.

GOD IS NEAR THE HUMBLE.
GOD IS FAR FROM THE PROUD.

(Joshua 23:24)

When Joshua got old, the people of Israel had changed: they had left behind the times of slavery in Egypt, of eating only manna or having no possessions. Now they had plenty; the problem was that some began to forget God just because they had so much. Joshua got their attention and told them to remember God, and told them that whatever they chose to do, he and his house would always serve the Lord.

 Question for us: Is it easier to pray to God when we have very little or when we have a lot?

 Knowing God better: Let's not forget to seek God when things are going well in our family. All families experience good and bad times. Let's seek God at all times.

GOD PROVIDES.
GOD KEEPS HIS PROMISES.

 Main characters:
Joshua: the conquering leader.
Caleb: even as an old man he kept conquering.

 Recommendation of verse to memorize:
Joshua 1:9

Have I not commanded you? Be strong and courageous. Do not be afraid; do not be discouraged, for the Lord your God will be with you wherever you go.

What other verses would you add?

_____   _____
_____   _____
_____   _____

 Download the "Family Readings and Conversations" from:
www.e625.com/lessons

Lesson 6 > JUDGES

General information about the book
Judges tells the stories of the leaders that God gave to the people of Israel to take care of themselves.
It has 21 chapters.

Who wrote it and in what era?
It is assumed that the writer of Judges was Samuel. It focuses on a time when there was still no king in Israel. That is why it is said that the book was written before 1043 BC, the date that Saul's reign begins.

Purpose of the book
Judges is the book that describes the authority delegated by God to these characters He anointed. Rather than reign, they were the voice of God for the people. The book covers about three hundred and fifty years, from the conquest of Joshua to the reign of King Saul.

Introductory activity
Fold a sheet of paper in half eight times. Try to tear that sheet. Do you find it impossible? Unfold it until you find when you can tear it.

Let's connect: Today we will tell several stories of men and women of faith.

Initial discussion:
Do you know who is recognized as an extremely strong man in the Bible? His story is one of disobedience and obedience. Today we will tell it.

What do we learn about God in this book?

(Judges 6:11-23)
Gideon was sitting under an oak tree, worried because he thought that the people of Israel were about to be conquered again, by the people of Midian. Meanwhile an angel was watching him. The angel says: "God is with you, mighty warrior!" Gideon stared at him and said: "Who, me? I am the smallest, of the smallest tribe."

Definitely Gideon did not feel like the chosen one. But the angel told him that if God was with him, he was the right choice. As he did not feel capable, he asked God three times for a miraculous sign three times. God had compassion on him and granted his request.

God worked through Gideon, and did not allow him to fight with a large army. He told him to choose an army of only three hundred men.

God gave Gideon a very creative strategy. He told each man to take a trumpet and a burning torch, covered with an empty jar. In the dark, the Israelites surrounded the camp of their enemies. At Gideon's signal, he and his men blew their trumpets, broke the jars and screamed. The enemies were consumed by great fear, thinking it was a huge army, and God gave the Israelites the victory.

 Question for us: Have you ever been too afraid or felt too small to do a task? (For example, when participating in a tournament, planning a project, or singing in public).

 Knowing God better: God can use us even if we feel too weak to do a task. Let us give our weakness and smallness to God so that He can show us his power through that in which we are small.

GOD IS MERCIFUL.
GOD IS ENOUGH FOR US.

(Judges 13 to 23)

Samson was born as a strong man who lived to save Israel from the Philistines. God told his mother that she should separate him for Him and that he should not allow his hair to be cut, because that was the sign that Samson was from God.

Samson grew strong but since he was very young, he began to trust in his strength. He was able to destroy a lion with his bare hands. He liked riddles a lot.

Samson fell in love with a Philistine girl whose name was Delilah. The Philistines told Delilah to find out from him the secret of his strength. Samson constantly tricked them, but she was getting closer and closer to discovering his secret.

Delilah began to bother Samson every day by saying, "If you love me, then you will tell me your secret." Samson could not stand her insistence and finally told her.

Then the Philistines knew how to defeat him, and they cut all his hair! Captured, and without strength, Samson was taken to a Philistine party for everyone to make fun of him. They took out his eyes. How sad for Samson! But the Philistines did not realize that Samson's hair had begun to grow again. Samson asked a boy to take him to the temple columns, and there he prayed to God to give him strength once again, in order to fulfill his mission of destroying the Philistines. He pushed the columns and destroyed the temple, with all the Philistines inside. Unfortunately, Samson also died that day.

 Question for us: What would you do if someone asked you to do something wrong to show them that you love them?

 Knowing God better: Samson's problem was that he played with bad things, thinking that they were not going to hurt him. For example, there are videos on the internet that do not teach us good things, and we watch them and say, "Nothing will happen to me." Let's be careful about what our eyes see and about who we associate with.

GOD IS MERCIFUL.

 Main characters:
Othniel: first Judge of Israel.
Deborah: only female judge.
Gideon: fifth judge of Israel, defeated the Midianites.
Abimelech: Gideon's evil son.
Samson: strong man dedicated to God.
Delilah: the woman who cheated Samson.

 Recommendation of verse to memorize:
Judges 6:12
The Lord is with you, mighty warrior.

What other verses would you add?

_____   _____
_____   _____
_____   _____

 Download the "Family Readings and Conversations" from:
www.e625.com/lessons

Lesson 7 > 1ST AND 2ND SAMUEL

General information about the book
These books tell us about the establishment of the kings.
1 Samuel has 31 chapters.
2 Samuel has 24 chapters.

Who wrote it and in what era?
These books were written by the prophet Samuel. After the era when the judges led the people by speaking for God, we moved on to the age of the kings.

Purpose of the book
The people wanted God to establish a king like the other people had, and then they choose their king, first Saul and then David. The emphasis is on Samuel's ministry and David's life.

Introductory activity
Using paper balls we will play target shooting. Let's test our aim. You can try to knock down empty cups or bottles.

Let's connect: Having good aim is not easy. Today we are going to talk about several Israeli kings. The most famous king was David, who knocked down a giant with one stone. Imagine what great aim he had! It was definitely God who directed that stone.

Initial discussion:
How do you imagine was David's sling?

What do we learn about God in these books?

(1st Samuel 15:1-16:13)
God had chosen Saul as king, but when he saw his bad behavior he repented, and appointed the prophet Samuel to look for a new king. He went to look for him at the house of Jesse, a man who had seven children. When he arrived he called the eldest son, who looked great and thought he was going to be the king. The Lord told Samuel that it was not him, and not to notice the outside because God looked at the heart. So he went through the second and the third, until he reached the seventh son.

Becoming sad, Samuel asked Jesse if he didn't have another child. Jesse replied that he also had a very young son who took care of the sheep. That son's name was David. He was called, and when Samuel saw him the Lord said: "He is the anointed one."

 Question for us: Have you ever judged someone by their appearance, and when you got to know them them you realized that they were a better person (or vice versa)?

 Knowing God better: God does not judge us by our appearance. He sees our heart, and treats us accordingly. Let's try to see people based on their heart and not on their appearance.

GOD SEES BEYOND WHAT WE SEE.

(1st Samuel 17:1-50)

After David was anointed, some time passed before he became king. The most famous story about David was the time he defeated the giant Goliath, by knocking him down with a stone. The story tells us that they wanted David to wear Saul's armor, which was very heavy. David decided not to wear Saul's armor, and to fight his own way. From that time on, Saul began to get increasingly jealous of David and to persecute him. Instead of trying to defend himself or get revenge, David decided not to disrespect the king, and to allow God to take care of installing him in his place.

 Question for us: What are the things at which God made you good?

 Knowing God better: Wearing another person's armor means wanting to act with the abilities of others. We must understand that there are things at which we are not naturally good, but there are others for which God gave us more talent. We shouldn't try to look like others just because they are more popular. Let's use the talents that God gave us.

GOD IS WISE.

(2nd Samuel 12:1-25)

When David became king, he was a great king; under his reign Israel prospered. But one day he had a problem: instead of going to a battle he stayed to rest at his palace. He saw a married woman who was not his wife and wanted to make her his wife. He thought that as a king he could send the woman's husband to battle to die in combat, and then he could stay with her. That is exactly what happened, and her husband died. Then David was able to make her his wife.

David thought that no one would notice, and he'd be able to hide what he had done. What a terrible time it was for David, trying to hide his sin! Nothing is hidden from God's eyes.

The Lord sent the prophet Nathan and confronted David with his sin. David repented, began to cry deeply, and asked the Lord for forgiveness. The Lord forgave him, but his mistake had consequences and his new wife lost the son she was expecting. We hurt ourselves deeply by hiding a sin from God.

 Question for us: How do we feel when we hide some mischief or a sin we have committed?

 Knowing God better: In spite of our errors, God is merciful, and he will always forgive us if we confess our mistakes. We spend a lot of time in anguish and suffering by hiding our errors. Let us seek God and ask him to forgive our sins through Jesus.

GOD IS FORGIVING.
GOD IS OMNISCIENT.

 Main characters
Eli: the priest who trained Samuel.
Hannah: Samuel's mother.
Samuel: priest and prophet.
Saul: first king of Israel.
Jonathan: Saul's son.
David: the greatest king of Israel.
Nathan: David's prophet and advisor.

Recommendation of verse to memorize:

1st Samuel 3:10
Speak, Lord, for your servant is listening

What other verses would you add?

_____   _____

_____   _____

_____   _____

 Download the "Family Readings and Conversations" from:
www.e625.com/lessons

Lesosn 8 › JOB

General information about the book
The book has the name of its main character. The central idea is that even the righteous can suffer.
Job has 42 chapters.

Who wrote it and in what era?
It is not known exactly who the author of Job was, or at what time it was written. Some say it may have been Moses, and others suggest it may have been Solomon.

Purpose of the book
To teach us that even people who are just can go through difficult situations. We want to find reasons why there is suffering, but sometimes there are no reasons, and all we have left with is to trust God.

Introductory activity
Tickle contest
Let us pretend that tickling is like a form of suffering. We are going to have a tickle contest, to see who can tolerate the most.

Let's connect: Sometimes we can't stand the suffering, and we are quick to get angry or disappointed, and we want to give up. Job is going to teach us that despite his suffering he never stopped believing in God.

Initial discussion:
When have you abandoned a race, or quit a project, because you couldn't go through it until the end?

What do we learn about God in this book?

(Job 1-42)
Job was a righteous man who had everything: a good family, money, health, houses and food. Satan said that Job worshiped God because he had everything. God told him that he trusted his son, and knew that he would follow him even if he didn't have all those things.

Job went through lots of suffering, and his whole life changed. He lost his money, his health and his family. He lost everything. Despite his suffering and seeing that his friends would not help him, Job remained faithful to God. His friends sought to accuse him over his situation, as they believed that Job must have done something very bad, and that was the reason why he was suffering. But Job never stopped trusting God. After he passed the test, Job forgave his friends and prayed for them. The Lord returned everything he had lost, and gave him twice what he'd previously had.

 Question for us: What is our attitude towards God when we are having a difficult time? For example, it may be our inability to pass a class at school, or perhaps something more difficult, like an illness or the loss of a loved one.

 Knowing God better: God is good and He will never leave us, but we must trust Him during times of difficulty.

GOD IS FAITHFUL.
GOD BELIEVES IN US.

 Main characters
Job: just man, patient in times of suffering.
Eliphaz, Bilbad and Zophar: Job's friends, who believed that Job had done something wrong that justified his suffering.

Recommendation of verse to memorize:

Job 1:21
The Lord gave and the Lord has taken away; may the name of the Lord be praised.

What other verses would you add?

_____   _____

_____   _____

_____   _____

 Download the "Family Readings and Conversations" from:
www.e625.com/lessons

Lesson 9 > PSALMS

General information about the book
The book of praises and songs of a nation.
It has 150 chapters.

Who wrote it and in what era?
We can identify more than seven songwriters. King David wrote at least seventy-five psalms. The sons of Korah at least ten, and Asaph twelve. Other authors include Solomon, Moses and Henan.

Purpose of the book
This book is a collection of the songs of the nation of Israel. They express human feelings and worship of God. We have the lyrics of these songs, but we don't have their music.

Introductory activity
Let's write a song with the following words, and then listen to how it sounds. We can set whatever beat we want to it. If we can do it in groups, all the better.

The words are:
Thank you
Love
Jesus
Morning
Galaxy
Surprise
Connect
Impressed

Let's connect: It is beautiful to be able to sing to God. When we sing we can be praying and talking with our Lord.

Initial discussion:
What kind of songs do you enjoy worshipping God with?

What do we learn about God in this book?

There are different types of psalms. Some these types are:
Psalms offering advice (1, 37 and 119).

Psalms about pain (3, 17, 120).
Psalms about trust (23, 90).
Psalms about royalty (2, 21, 144).
Psalms of thanks (19, 32, 111).

 Question for us: Think about the most important thing that happened to you this week (difficult or happy). What type of psalm do you want to use, based on the event that you chose?

 Knowing God better: Many times we can use the psalms to learn to pray to God, or to receive advice from God for a specific situation.

GOD IS NEAR.

(Psalms 23)

Let's study Psalm 23, one of the most famous psalms.

1 The Lord is my shepherd, I lack nothing.
2 He makes me lie down in green pastures,
he leads me beside quiet waters,
3 he refreshes my soul.
He guides me along the right paths
for his name's sake.
4 Even though I walk
through the darkest valley,
I will fear no evil,
for you are with me;
your rod and your staff,
they comfort me.
5 You prepare a table before me
in the presence of my enemies.
You anoint my head with oil;
my cup overflows.
6 Surely your goodness and love will follow me
all the days of my life,
and I will dwell in the house of the Lord
forever.

Question for us: Which of the six verses do you like the most?

 Knowing God better: We challenge you to learn the verse that you chose. Find the people who have chosen the other verses that you didn't choose, and when you find them, say the whole psalm out loud as a team.

GOD IS OUR SHEPHERD.

(Psalms 150)

Now let's study this other psalm:

1 Praise the Lord.
Praise God in his sanctuary;
praise him in his mighty heavens.
2 Praise him for his acts of power;
praise him for his surpassing greatness.
3 Praise him with the sounding of the trumpet,
praise him with the harp and lyre.
4 praise him with timbrel and dancing,
praise him with the strings and pipe,
5 praise him with the clash of cymbals,
praise him with resounding cymbals.
6 Let everything that has breath praise the Lord.
Praise the Lord.

How about if we make a loud noise with whatever we have close to us, to praise God?

 Question for us: Why do you want to praise God today?

 Knowing God better: Our God is worthy of praise. All of us who have life and who breathe should praise God and be grateful for life, for health, for food, for his love, for friends, for family, and for so many other things for which we can give thanks.

GOD IS WORTHY OF PRAISE.

 Main characters
David: king of Israel; The writer of a majority of these psalms.

Recommendation of verse to memorize:

Psalms 90:1
Lord, you have been our dwelling place throughout all generations.

What other verses would you add?

_____   _____

_____   _____

_____   _____

Download the "Family Readings and Conversations" from:
www.e625.com/lessons

Lesson 10 > PROVERBS

General information about the book
It's also called Proverbs of Solomon.
It has 31 chapters.

Who wrote it and in what era?
It was probably written by Solomon, who also gathered the proverbs of other wise men. It dates from the time when Solomon ruled, before his heart turned away from God.

Purpose of the book
To share wisdom in order to enable us to make the right decisions.

Introductory activity
Using a paper Bible, we will compete to find the following proverbs. Whoever finds it first will read it out loud.

Proverbs 19:18
Proverbs 19:8
Proverbs 18:24
Proverbs 18:21
Proverbs 18:9
Proverbs 1:7
Proverbs 21:4
Proverbs 12:15
Proverbs 13:17

Let's connect: There is so much wisdom in the book of Proverbs! If you want to acquire wisdom, this is a good place to start.

Initial discussion:
Which of the proverbs we've read can you remember?

What do we learn about God in this book?

Wisdom (PROVERBS 2:1-6)

Read Proverbs 2, verses 1 through 6, and you will see that God wants to give us wisdom. The Lord is the one who gives wisdom. If we look for it and ask for it, He will give it to us. But searching for wisdom cannot be simple. We must strive to find it.

 Question for us: How can we show God that we really want wisdom?

 Knowing God better: If we strive for wisdom, God will give it to us. It is a precious object. What do you do with something that has a lot of value? You take care of it. The same goes for wisdom.

GOD IS WISDOM.

Fools

The book of Proverbs teaches us that the opposite of wise people are foolish, mocking and lazy people. The fool is one who does not want to change his bad behavior. In fact, when someone tries to correct him, he is always looking for someone to blame. The mocker is the one who laughs at the expense of the pain or problems of others. Mocking people don't end well, according to the book of proverbs. Lazy people do not achieve much in life, they are always looking for excuses to avoid doing things. Honest work is blessed by the Lord. If you want wisdom, stay away from being foolish, mocking or lazy.

Read Proverbs 26; It explains well this kind of people.

 Question for us: We all fight to avoid becoming one of these three types of people. With which behavior (foolish, mocking or lazy) have you had more problems?

 Knowing God better: Although we can all fall into being foolish, mocking or lazy, we must focus on seeking more of God's wisdom. If we ask God for wisdom, He will give it to us. But we must strive to get it and take care of it.

If our parents correct us, we must understand that they do it because they love us and want us to learn to become wise people, who can make good decisions.

GOD IS WISE.
GOD CORRECTS US, BUT HE LOVES US.

Main characters
Solomon: son of David; called the wise king.

Recommendation of verse to memorize:

Proverbs 22:6

Start children off on the way they should go, and even when they are old they will not turn from it.

What other verses would you add?

_____   _____
_____   _____
_____   _____

Download the "Family Readings and Conversations" from:
desde www.e625.com/lessons

Lesson 11> ECCLESIASTES AND SONG OF SONGS

General information about the book

Ecclesiastes is also called the book of the preacher.
The Song of Songs is a book that represents the best song written by Solomon.
Ecclesiastes has 12 chapters and Songs of Songs has 8.

Who wrote it and in what era?

These books were most likely written by king Solomon. They were written during the reign of King Solomon, who asked God for wisdom in order to rule his people.

Purpose of the book

The purpose of the book of Ecclesiastes is to answer the most challenging life questions. It considers what is really important in life, and concludes that what is most important is our relationship with and dependence on God.
In Song of Songs, Solomon writes a love song.

Introductory activity

Using these seven words make a poem where you express love for Jesus.
> Thanks
> Lantern
> Potato
> Ball
> Heart
> Star
> Sum

Let's connect: We can express our love by singing to God. Songs, poems and art in general can serve us to express our love for God.

Initial discussion:

Which type of art would you like the most to express your love for God? (Singing, dancing, sculptures, writing, making movies, etc.).

What do we learn about God in this book?

ECCLESIASTES

According to Solomon, all life is vanity (empty, meaningless) unless we recognize that it comes from God's hand. He says that fame, success, trophies and all those things can be vanity if we don't understand that it is God who gives them to us.

According to Solomon these are some of the most common vanities of people:

    Human wisdom (Ecclesiastes 2: 14-16)
    Human effort (Ecclesiastes 2: 18-23)
    Human triumphs (Ecclesiastes 2:26)
    Human rivalries (Ecclesiastes 4: 4)
    Human power (Ecclesiastes 4:16)
    Human greed (Ecclesiastes 5:10)
    Accumulation of goods (Ecclesiastes 6: 1-12)

 Question for us: What do you understand by vanity, and what do you think is the most common vanity people have?

 Knowing God better: God wants to bless us, and he gives us victories, things and happiness, for us to enjoy wisely. The problem comes when we put first in our lives those things that God gives us, and use them only for ourselves; We fail to understand that God gave these things to us so we can help others and share with them.

GOD IS HE WHO BLESSES US.

According to Ecclesiastes 3, there is a time for everything. Time to study and time to rest, time to eat and time to play. Solomon is trying to tell us that nothing can take all our time. For example, playing video games can be enjoyable for a while, but if it takes all our time it becomes an obsession, and that doesn't please God.

 Question for us: What do you spend most of your time on?

 Knowing God better: You have to know how to manage your time well. Understand that there is a time for everything. How you invest your time says a lot about what will happen to you when you grow up.

A swimmer invests his time in swimming, someone intelligent invests it in studying, someone lazy ... how do you think he invests it?

GOD IS OUR GREATEST VICTORY.

SONG OF SONGS

When two people love each other, they write songs, poems or do nice things to please each other. Our greatest love is for God. The Song of Songs is an example of how the love of two people can be compared to the love we have for God.

 Question for us: What are your reasons for wanting to sing to God?

 Knowing God better: When we sing to God, we are talking with Him through music. Singing to God is a good way to offer prayers for God.

GOD IS LOVE.

 Main characters
In Ecclesiastes:
The preacher: the one who writes the book.
In the Song of Songs:
The beloved (he): Believed to be Solomon.
The beloved (she): Solomon's wife.

 Recommendation of verse to memorize:

Ecclesiastes 12:1
Remember your Creator in the days of your youth, before the days of trouble come.

What other verses would you add?

_____ _____
_____ _____
_____ _____

 Download the "Family Readings and Conversations" from:
www.e625.com/lessons

Lesson 12 > AMOS

General information about the book
Known as one of the minor prophets of the Old Testament, due to the short content of his book.
It has 9 chapters.

Who wrote it and in what era?
This book mentions the prophet Amos. Unlike others, he is not a member of a family of priests; He is a farmer. He is known as a shepherd, and someone who worked with figs. He wrote during the reign of Uzziah, king of Judah, and Jeroboam II, king of Israel.

Purpose of the book
Amos focuses on the sins committed by the people. He gets their attention and challenges them to repent. He reminds them that there is hope! But they must stop their injustice. During that time the people were enjoying economic prosperity, but they were oppressing the poor. This was not a reflection of God's character.

Introductory activity
Let's plan a game with balloons, volleyball style. Let's form two teams and mark the playing area. The rules are very simple: if the balloon falls within the territory of a team, it is a point for the adversary. They can touch the globe as many times as they want and use all parts of the body. There is only a small variant: one of the teams will have to play with their hands tied behind their backs; The other team will have their hands loose.

Let's connect: In this activity a team was the clear winner because the conditions were unfair. It is very easy to take advantage of, and even make fun of, those who do not have the same possibilities as we do. In everyday life, the same could happen to those who find themselves in less favorable situations than ours.

Initial discussion:
How do you think God expects us to act towards people who are suffering or have fewer opportunities than us? How does God treat each of us?

What do we learn about God in this book?

(AMOS 1:6,7a)

At the beginning of the chapter we see God roaring (1: 2). This lion symbol makes us think of the threat of a terrible danger; the lion that is ready to attack its prey. God uses this symbol to alert his people. They were very comfortable living in sin, and God warns them that they should be afraid. If they did not repent, the punishment would come. One of the people's many sins was being very cruel to the poor. We see that, for example, if someone borrowed money to buy a pair of shoes and then could not pay the debt, the rich would take advantage of this to sell them as slaves. They had no compassion!

 Question for us: How can we show mercy towards those who don't have as much as we do?

 Knowing God better: God expects his people to behave just as He would behave; the children of God must closely resemble their father, God! In this book we are reminded that God is not someone who takes advantage of the poor without mercy; rather, he wants to defend the rights of the poor.

GOD IS JUST AND LOVES JUSTICE.

(AMOS 1:1-15 and 2:1-5)

Amos begins by pronouncing judgments for several nations. Notice how many of these are mentioned in chapters 1 and 2 (1:3,6,9,11,13; 2:1,4). Several cities are mentioned and details are given of the severity of the punishment. They will not be able to escape.

Perhaps many Jews were happy to read about this, because the nations mentioned were indeed cruel, and in addition they were their enemies. It is very easy to rejoice when there is judgment and punishment for our enemies! It is so easy to think that they deserve it because they are evil. However, just after this narration, the judgement for Israel is mentioned. They had also turned away from obedience to God.

 Question for us: What comes easier? Judging others or judging ourselves?

 Knowing God better: God is just, and He wants everyone to recognize their sin and repent. We must help others to see their faults, but mainly we must be very aware of our own. Our hope to be forgiven is not to try harder (we will always fail!); Our only hope is in Jesus, who forgives us completely.

GOD EXAMINES US, AND GIVES A SOLUTION TO OUR PROBLEM.

(AMOS 9:11-15)

The entire book of Amos talks about judgment and punishment. It seems like the good news will never come! But God is always a God of hope. At the end of the book, Amos pronounces prophecies that refer to Jesus, the Messiah, descendant of David. God promises that there will be restoration, because He will fulfill what he has promised.

 Question for us: Do you find it hard to believe that a promise will be fulfilled, when it appears to be taking a long time?

 Knowing God better: Despite his people's disobedience, God remains their protector and provider. Above all, He remains faithful and will fulfill what He has promised. He wants his people to know Him and make Him known to others as well.

GOD FULFILLS ALL HIS PROMISES.

 Main characters
Amos: prophet, shepherd, farmer.
Amaziah: priest who wanted to prevent Amos from continuing to prophesy.
Israel: the kingdom to which the book is directed.

 Recommendation of verse to memorize:
Amos 5:24

But let justice roll on like a river, righteousness like a never-failing stream

What other verses would you add?

_____ _____
_____ _____
_____ _____

 Download the "Family Readings and Conversations" from:
www.e625.com/lessons

Lesson 13 > OBADIAH AND JOEL

General information about the book
Obadiah is the book in which God judges the enemies of Israel.
Joel is about the day of the Lord.
Obadiah has 1 chapter.
Joel has 3 chapters.

Who wrote it and in what era?
Both books seem to have been written by the prophets mentioned in them.
Obadiah was probably from the same era as Elijah and Elisha, while Joel's time
is unknown.

Purpose of the book
Obadiah lived in Jerusalem after the exile of Judah to Babylon. He was the messen-
ger of God who announced the fall of the Edomites, who were the descendants of
Esau, and had rejoiced when Judah fell. He also prophesied of a future when the
Jews would once again rule the lands that had once been under David's control.

Joel's book is divided into two parts; (1) a great calamity caused by a locust inva-
sion, and (2) God's response to the prayers of the people. The book contains a
prophecy that is frequently found in the writings of the prophets: that the Jews
would establish a great nation in Palestine in the future.

Introductory activity
Who will drop the ball? We form a a circle and throw a small ball (like a tennis
ball) to a teammate who is not next to us. If the ball is dropped, we have to start
over and follow the same route, so they must memorize the route. We will do it
with several teams, and we will compete to see which team can do it faster.

Let's connect: Who had the most difficulty playing the game? What was
the attitude of the group towards them?

Initial discussion:
God rewards compassion, and hates egotism and pride.

What do we learn about God in this book?

(Obadiah 1:12)

The book of Obadiah is the shortest in the Old Testament. It only has one chapter, but it brings us a great message. The book refers to the story of Esau and Jacob. Remember? Esau was the one who sold his birthright to Jacob for a plate of lentils. Esau always held a grudge and treated Jacob poorly. In this book the prophet Obadiah tells us how things will not go well for the descendants of Esau, for having treated Jacob's descendants poorly.

Question for us: Have you ever felt bad because you were laughed at?

Knowing God better: Never laugh at your brother or someone at close to you to mock them. In fact, we should never laugh in a mocking way at anyone, much less at our brothers.

GOD IS JUST

(Joel 2:13)

The Lord is slow to get angry and full of love. When our parents get mad at us, they do it because we have done something wrong. The truth is that they don't like to get angry, but they do it to make us understand that we need to be punished and not do it again. The Lord is good, even more so than our parents, and desires the best for us, even when that means he must scold us.

Imagine if after we have done a great mischief, we apologized to our parents. They may decide to forgive us, and still give us a gift because they love us …. That would be very nice, right? The prophet Joel was telling the people of Israel something like that.

The prophet Joel told the people of Israel to seek forgiveness from the Lord, trusting that God is slow to be angry and full of love. He told them that God can change his mind, reconsider his punishment, and even give us a blessing (undeserved).

Question for us: Have you ever been guilty of some mischief and your parents decided to forgive you?

 Knowing God better: If our parents, who are not as good as God, decide to forgive us, how much more will our Lord, who is extremely good, decide to forgive us, when we repent and ask Him to forgive us?

GOD IS MERCY
GOD IS SLOW TO ANGER
GOD IS FULL OF LOVE

 Main characters
In the Book of Obadiah:
Edomites: a nation that descends from Esau, judged by God.
In the Book of Joel:
Joel: prophet to the people of Judah during the time of Joash.
The people of Judah: The southern kingdom, punished by God with a plague of locusts.

 Recommendation of verse to memorize:
JOEL 2:13
    Rend your heart
    and not your garments.
    Return to the Lord your God,
    for he is gracious and compassionate,
    slow to anger and abounding in love,
    and he relents from sending calamity.

What other verses would you add?

_____   _____
_____   _____
_____   _____

 Download the "Family Readings and Conversations" from:
www.e625.com/lessons

Lesson 14 > RUTH

General information about the book
It is a love story that took place during the time of the Judges.
Ruth has 4 chapters.

Who wrote it and in what era?
It is believed that the author of this book was Samuel. It was written shortly before, or during, David's reign in Israel.

Purpose of the book
This book has been called one of the best examples of a short narrative ever written. It's a story of faith and mercy during the time of the judges. It tells us about the life of Naomi and her daughter-in-law Ruth (who was an ancestor of King David, and of Jesus).

Introductory activity
We are going to have a wheat stalk harvesting race. Wheat stalks (or objects that simulate them) will be randomly placed in a room The challenge is to try to get the most stalks, with the challenge of being able to jump only on one foot. The one who collects the most stalks wins.

Let's connect: Ruth made a living collecting stalks in the field of Boaz, who later became her husband.

Initial discussion:
How difficult do you think it is to collect stalks? How long do you think you would endure if you had to do it throughout the day? The Bible says that Boaz was astonished at Ruth because she worked very hard. People notice how hard you try, even if you don't realize it.

What do we learn about God in this book?

Ruth 2
Ruth's husband died, and she stayed with her mother-in-law Naomi. Naomi's pain was twofold. She had lost his son (Ruth's husband), and she had no one to work to feed her and Ruth. So Ruth decided to go to work in the fields of a very rich person (Boaz). When Boaz saw her work so hard, he was impressed, because he saw that she was not only working for her, but also for her mother-in-law, whom she didn't want to leave alone. The work was very hard: she had to pick up stalks all day long in the sun.

Question for us: Have you ever been rewarded for your efforts?

 Knowing God better: Working hard and being rewarded for it is gratifying, but it is more gratifying when our work also benefits others. Your parents are a good example of working hard to benefit someone else. It would be a good idea to give your parents a hug for all the effort they are making for you.

GOD IS HE WHO REWARDS..

Ruth 3-4

Boaz fell in love with Ruth, because of her effort and the way she helped Naomi. Ruth never imagined that this effort would save her, because after feeling alone, with no one to take care of her and no food, Boaz asked her to be his wife, and they got married. Now Ruth and Naomi lived happily and with many things to enjoy.

Boaz and Ruth had a son named Obed, who was the father of Jesse, who had eight children, the youngest of whom was named David (who became king). Imagine how much God can reward a person's effort, even if at the time the work seems hard and complicated.

 Question for us: What do you think is the lesson we learn from the book of Ruth?

 Knowing God better: When we go through a difficult and complicated time, during which we have no choice but to strive to get ahead, we have the assurance that the Lord will reward that effort and that we will enjoy its benefits for a long time. Studying for a difficult math test can be hard, but perhaps in the future you will become a great scientist, and save many lives! Your effort can take you far!

GOD IS IN CONTROL OF OUR LIVES.

Main characters
Naomi: mother-in-law of Ruth.
Ruth: the protagonist of the story.
Boaz: a rich man who marries Ruth.
Obed: son of Ruth and Boaz, grandfather of King David.

Recommendation of verse to memorize:

Ruth 2:12

May you be richly rewarded by the Lord, the God of Israel, under whose wings you have come to take refuge

What other verses would you add?

_____   _____
_____   _____
_____   _____

Download the "Family Readings and Conversations" from:
www.e625.com/lessons

Lesson 15 > ISAIAH

General information about the book
Isaiah is one of the major prophets. His name means "the Lord saves."
It has 66 chapters.

Who wrote it and in what era?
Isaiah wrote it during difficult times. The people had turned away from the Lord and had done evil. It is the most mentioned book in the New Testament.

Purpose of the book
Isaiah was one of the most important prophets, a contemporary of other prophets, like Hosea and Micah. He wrote with elegance and lots of creativity, using a large vocabulary (more than 2,186 words). The emphasis of this book is on its prophecies about the coming of Jesus as the Messiah and Savior.

Introductory activity
Walking blindfolded
We will divide into teams. Each team will choose a person to blindfold. Then we will place five objects per team distributed throughout the room. Each team will guide the blindfolded person with five instructions: forward, backward, right, left, higher. The first team to collect the five items and return to where it started will win.

Let's connect: In the Old Testament the prophets functioned as guides with God's voice who directed the steps of the people of Israel. We often need people who speak to us on God's behalf, because we cannot see things as clearly as God sees them.

Initial discussion:
Through which people in your life has God spoken to you to guide you?

What do we learn about God in this book?

Scolding and good news (Isaiah 1-9)
The Lord used the prophet Isaiah to talk about the terrible things the people had done, and to tell them that no one would escape punishment, unless they turned away from evil. He told them: "Tell God that you repent, before it's too late." Sadly, nobody wanted to hear the bad news.

But Isaiah also had good news. He told the people: "God will punish his people because they don't listen to him. But he won't be angry forever. He will remember them."

He announced that he would give them his Son, who was going to bring light into the darkness. This child would be born from the family of King David, and God's spirit would be with Him. This child is Jesus.

 Question for us: What happens when God speaks to us through people and we do not obey? Can we see God's love in His punishment?

 Knowing God better: The Bible says that God loves us and he corrects those He loves. He corrects us because he loves us and because we are his children. When we see that our parents correct us because we do not obey them, we see that they do it because they love us. The best way to live intelligently and with less pain is to listen to God when he corrects us, and do what He asks us to do.

GOD IS CREATOR.

Isaiah announces Jesus

Isaiah announces to the Savior and the Messiah, the one the people of Israel were waiting for. He announces the deliverer. When you read, for example, chapter 61 you realize that he is talking about Jesus. Imagine, this book was written 700 years before Jesus came!

Isaiah announced the boy and said what we would call him: "For unto us a child is born, unto us a son is given, and the government will be upon His shoulders. And He will be called Wonderful Counselor, Mighty God, Everlasting Father, Prince of Peace."

We thank God for having sent Jesus to us.

 Question for us: What does each of the names that Isaiah said we would call Jesus mean to you?

 Knowing God better: God guides us by counseling us; He fills us with faith because we know that He is strong and almighty; He makes us feel loved because we know that he is our father, He always has been and always will be, and He fills our life with peace as a very precious gift in difficult times.

GOD IS ADMIRABLE, STRONG, ETERNAL FATHER AND PRINCE OF PEACE.

Main characters

Isaiah: prophet of God; His message was one of judgment and of hope.

Recommendation of verse to memorize:

Isaiah 54:10
Though the mountains be shaken and the hills be removed, yet my unfailing love for you will not be shaken nor my covenant of peace be removed, says the LORD, who has compassion on you.

What other verses would you add?

_____   _____

_____   _____

_____   _____

**Download the "Family Readings and Conversations" from:
www.e625.com/lessons**

Lesson 16 > EZEKIEL

General information about the book
A book that reflects the glory of God.
It has 48 chapters.

Who wrote it and in what era?
It was written by Ezekiel, who was twenty-five years old when he was taken captive and thirty when he was called into the ministry (that was the age at which the priests began their office). The book was written between 593 and 550 B.C.

Purpose of the book
Ezekiel was young when he was taken into captivity. The theme of his prophecy is the destruction of Jerusalem, the judgment on the people and, finally, the return of the exiles and the glorious future of Israel.

Introductory activity
Speaking with signs (the mimicry game)
We will form teams. Each team will choose a member who will have some keywords (And it's best if they are related to the parables from the book of Ezekiel, for example "dry bones"). They will stand in front, and only with mimics (without speaking) they will describe the word. Their team's challenge will be to try to figure out what word he is describing.

> **Let's connect:** Ezekiel had a very particular style of speaking on behalf of God. He did it by using examples, parables and even mimics.

Initial discussion:
God speaks to us by various means and in various ways. Sometimes he speaks with words but sometimes he speaks through examples. How would you tell a friend that "I can do everything in Christ who strengthens me", without using written or spoken words?

What do we learn about God in this book?

Ezekiel's Signals
Ezekiel was a very peculiar prophet. He used different examples, signs, actions and even dramatizations in order to prophesy. Some of the signs he used were these:
Ezekiel had to shave his head and beard (Ezekiel 5: 1-4).
Ezekiel had to pack his things and dig to open a gap on the wall of Jerusalem (Ezekiel 12: 1-14).

Ezekiel had to eat bread while trembling and drink water while shivering (Ezekiel 12: 17-20).
Ezekiel had to sharpen a sword and smite one hand against the other (Ezekiel 21: 8-17).
Ezekiel was dumb for a while (Ezekiel 24: 25-27).
The prophet sought to explain why Jerusalem was going to face judgment and was going to be destroyed. But he did not finish there, as he also prophesied on God's behalf about the restoration of Israel.

He prophesied in many creative ways.

 Question for us: In what creative ways can we have to talk to others about God and tell them to do what's right?

 Knowing God better: Often people need a different or more graphic explanation to be able to receive a message. God is a creative God and has endowed us with lots of imagination and intelligence to enable us to help others understand his message.

GOD IS CREATIVE.

Dry bones (Ezekiel 37: 1-11)

Perhaps the most famous story in Ezekiel is that of the Valley of the Dry Bones. Ezekiel talks about a vision he had about a valley where there were only bones of people. I think it was like a cemetery. There, the Lord told him to prophesy so that the bones would become filled with flesh and skin. Imagine what that scene must have been like! Ezekiel complied, and God gave them flesh and skin. The problem with the regeneration of the bodies is that they still had no life. Then the Lord told Ezekiel to blow on them to give them life.

 Question for us: What do you think is the meaning of God asking Ezekiel to blow on the bodies?

 Knowing God better: A person without God in his heart needs to feel God's breath in him. The breath of God is his Holy Spirit. The Bible says that God is good and will give his Spirit to everyone who asks.

GOD IS HE WHO GIVES LIFE.

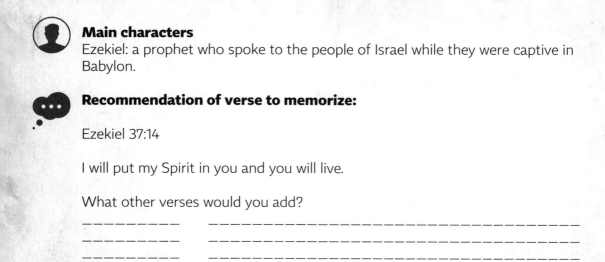

Main characters

Ezekiel: a prophet who spoke to the people of Israel while they were captive in Babylon.

Recommendation of verse to memorize:

Ezekiel 37:14

I will put my Spirit in you and you will live.

What other verses would you add?

_ _ _ _ _ _ _ _ _   _
_ _ _ _ _ _ _ _ _   _
_ _ _ _ _ _ _ _ _   _

Download the "Family Readings and Conversations" from:
www.e625.com/lessons

Lesson 17 > DANIEL

General information about the book
Daniel is the book of visions about the future.
It has 66 chapters.

Who wrote it and in what era?
The writer of the book is Daniel, whose name means "God is my judge." It was written during the Babylonian exile, after Jerusalem was conquered. The book begins in the year 605 B.C.

Purpose of the book
This is one of the most exciting books, in terms of its stories. This book talks about the empires and powers that have ruled the world, and is considered a vision about the end times.

Introductory activity
Serious face contest
In pairs, we will have a serious face contest. One person should make the other one laugh without touching him. If for a minute and a half he able to make him laugh, the other one wins. Players will be eliminated until the champion is the last one left.

Let's connect: Sometimes others want us to do things we don't want to do. In this game it was something fun and good, but sometimes they may encourage us to do bad things that we don't want to do. We must ask the Lord for strength to withstand the pressure of the group.

Initial discussion:
Who has been in a situation in which he felt pressured by the group to do something he did not want to do?

What do we learn about God in this book?

The Red Hot Furnace
King Nebuchadnezzar built a huge golden statue to which all people were ordered to bow down to and worship whenever the music played. There were three friends of Daniel whose names were Shadrach, Meshach, and Abednego, who refused to do so because they knew that they could only bow before God.

The whole **BIBLE** *in a year* **CHILDREN**

The king was very angry and had them brought to him. He told his men to throw them into a furnace of fire. The young men said it didn't matter, that God would deliver them from the fire. Moreover, they added that even if God decided not to deliver them, they would still worship God alone.

Indeed, when they were thrown into the fire everyone thought they had been burned, but when they looked through a small window, they saw a fourth man who was watching over them, and they did not burn. Then the king ordered to have them taken out immediately, and admitted that there is only one God who saves.

 Question for us: There are songs today that have very ugly lyrics. Would you be willing to decide not to listen to the music whose lyrics do not please God, despite the pressure of your group of friends?

 Knowing God better: God is powerful and able to keep us from any evil. When your friends who don't know God ask you to do something wrong, resist. God will always take care of you and will give you a way out.

GOD IS FAITHFUL.

The Madness of the Kings

Daniel interpreted a dream that King Nebuchadnezzar had, in which a tree that had grown a lot was cut and its leaves and fruits were uprooted. That dream meant that God was going to remove the king because he had become proud, believing himself bigger than God. Then the king went through a time of madness, but at the end of that time he recognized that God really was the Almighty, and praised God.

When the king died, Daniel and his friends were forgotten and another king came to reign. This new king, Belshazzar, forgot about God, and again God sent a warning to the king: a finger wrote on the wall some words that no one but Daniel could interpret. This time, although the king acknowledged that he was wrong, it was too late and he died that same day.

 Question for us: How does a proud person act? Have you ever acted like that?

70

Knowing God better: God tells us in the book of Daniel that He does not like proud and egotistical people. He gives them opportunities to change, but it is up to us to obey.

GOD IS MERCY.
GOD IS FAR AWAY FROM THE PROUD
AND CLOSE TO THE HUMBLE.

Daniel in the lions' den

Daniel served a new king. He was very good at what he did, so the kings always wanted him by their side. The king's other advisors were not happy about it, so they convinced the king that, in the next thirty days, no one should pray to anyone other than the king!

Of course, Daniel obeyed everything except that which was not right. The king, seeing that Daniel disobeyed him, decided as a punishment to throw him into a den with lions. The king really didn't want to do it, but he did it under pressure from his advisors. When they threw him he even said to Daniel: "Perhaps your God will save you." And what do you think happened? Indeed, God saved him. Daniel was left unharmed, and the king was glad and punished the men who had conspired against Daniel.

 Question for us: How far must we go to obey?

 Knowing God better: We must always obey our elders, until they ask us to do something that is not right before God.

GOD IS FAITHFUL.
GOD TAKES CARE OF US.

 Main characters
Daniel: counselor of the king.
Shadrach, Meshach, and Abednego: Daniel's friends, Righteous men before God.
King Nebuchadnezzar: great king of Babylon, he went mad for some time for not recognizing the sovereignty of God.
King Belshazzar: successor of Nebuchadnezzar; He also used Daniel as an interpreter. King Darius: succeeded Belshazzar as king.

Recommendation of verse to memorize:

Daniel 2:20
Praise be to the name of God for ever and ever;
wisdom and power are his.

What other verses would you add?

_____   _____
_____   _____
_____   _____

Download the "Family Readings and Conversations" from:
www.e625.com/lessons

Lesson 18 > JEREMIAH

General information about the book
It tells about the life and trials of the prophet Jeremiah, and his message to the people of God.
It has 52 chapters.

Who wrote it and in what era?
Jeremiah wrote this book. Jeremiah served as a priest and a prophet. Jeremiah is referred to as the weeping prophet. It was written around 600 B.C.

Purpose of the book
The prophet lived during sad times for the Hebrew people. He suffered greatly and unfairly. He wrote about God's judgment to a people who were sinned, but also wrote about the greatness of divine love.

Introductory activity
Using modeling clay we will be making several pots. The challenge is to form them while turning them. We cannot stop turning or moving the pots as we make them. If we want to stop, we must undo everything and start over.

Let's connect: In the book of Jeremiah, God compares us to pots made by a potter. To make the pots, the potter would spin them until they looked right. If they didn't turn out right, he would destroy them and start making them again.

Initial discussion:
Why do you think God compared us with pots hand-made by the potter?

What do we learn about God in this book?

It is not too late to repent (Jeremiah 2-17)
Jeremiah spoke to the people of Israel, reminding them about how God brought them out of Egypt, how they followed him and how He helped them when they asked for help.

God asked them why they've abandoned him to follow other idols. But he told them that it was not too late to repent. He told them: "It is not too late to return to me and keep the pact we made. Act now." The Lord asked them to show repentance. Unfortunately they ignored him.

 Question for us: What are the most frequent reasons why we forget God?

 Knowing God better: Anything that separates us from God and makes us do improper things works just as an idol like the ones that Jeremiah warned the people of Israel about. Let's consider if there is something that is separating us from following God. God's voice for us is: "It is not too late to repent."

GOD IS MERCIFUL.

Clay in the hands of the potter (Jeremiah 18: 1-20: 2)

God asked Jeremiah to go to the potter's house. There he stopped to watch the potter work on his lathe. It shaped some clay around it until it took the form of a pot. A lathe is a device that turns around so that the potter can mold the clay.

God told Jeremiah, "I am like the potter. My people are like this clay. If they are rebellious and disobedient, and they cannot be the nation I intended them to be, then I will begin again. "

 Question for us: What happens at school when you don't learn a subject well and don't pass it at the end of the year?

 Knowing God better: Just like at school, when we have to keep taking exams until we learn the lesson, God corrects us over and over until we learn what He wants to teach us.

GOD IS THE POTTER.

Main characters

Jeremiah: priest and prophet of the southern kingdom of Judah.
King Josiah: sixteenth king of Judah; He tried to follow God.
King Jehoahaz evil son of Josiah.
King Jehoiakim: evil son of Josiah.
King: Jehoiachin evil son of Jehoiakim.
King Zedekiah: evil uncle of Jehoiachin.
Baruch: served as scribe of Jeremiah.
Ebed-Melech: official who helped Jeremiah.

Recommendation of verse to memorize:

Jeremiah 29:11
For I know the plans I have for you," declares the Lord, "plans to prosper you and not to harm you, plans to give you hope and a future.

What other verses would you add?

_____   _____

_____   _____

_____   _____

Download the "Family Readings and Conversations" from:
www.e625.com/lessons

Lesson 19 > ZEPHANIAH

General information about the book
He is one of the minor prophets because of the short length of his book. It has 2 chapters.

Who wrote it and in what era?
It is written by a direct descendant of King Hezekiah, who prophesied during the reign of Josiah, who was the last king of Judah and one of the few who obeyed God. Zephaniah is contemporary of Jeremiah and Habakkuk.

Purpose of the book
Zephaniah reminds the people that they have broken the covenant with God, and that they must repent. But the people did not always obey, so they would often be punished to get them to react. However, there is always the promise of restoration and hope. The book speaks repeatedly about "the day of the Lord," and this means that the righteous God will have to punish the disobedience of those who have rejected Him.

Introductory activity
We will take sheets of paper to draw the most creative mask we can think of. We can use figures, colors, etc. Then, we will put on the mask, and without revealing anything we will try to guess what expression someone has behind the mask (it has to be different from the one others can see!). Then, everyone will show the true expression they hid behind the mask. We can take pictures of each one and give prizes for the funniest, the most serious, etc.

Let's connect: When we hide behind a mask nobody can see what we are really experiencing. We can appear to be a certain way, but the reality may be different. This is okay when playing a game, but it's not right when it comes to our spiritual life. We cannot deceive God by appearing to be something that is not real in our heart.

Initial discussion:
Do you think it is possible to pretend to be a child of God? Is it possible to hide disobedience from other people? From God?

What do we learn about God in this book?

(Zephaniah 1 1-6)

God's people pretended to be obedient to God, but in fact they had turned away from Him. Their rebellion was such that they blatantly worshiped other gods that were abominable. They thought it was okay for them to serve God and serve other pagan gods. However, God emphasized that he would destroy those gods and all who worshipped them. Why? Because He is the only true God.

 Question for us: What do you think it means to worship God? How do we do it?

 Knowing God better: There are many false gods, and it's very easy to fall and worship them. However, there is only one true God. That is why it is very offensive to Him when we give our worship to anything else.

GOD IS THE ONLY ONE WORTHY OF WORSHIP.

(Zephaniah 2 1-3)

To seek the Lord refers to us seeking Him, and repenting. It is the opposite of indifference or abandoning the Lord. The people of God were guilty of both, and therefore the Lord had also turned His back on them. However, genuinely seeking the Lord means seeking justice and humility.

 Question for us: What do you think it means to be humble before God?

 Knowing God better: God is always good, and constantly gives us new opportunities to repent and return to Him. No matter what we have done, He is able to and wants to forgive us. What He wants to see is a heart that recognizes that He is God and that we are his children; We must be obedient because we love Him.

GOD IS THE GOD OF NEW OPPORTUNITIES.

(Zephaniah 3 14:17)

Due to the people's evildoing, Zephaniah reminds them that there will be justice. They must yearn for their God and put their hope in Him. God's purpose is to gather a people to worship him. Therefore, they must rejoice in the salvation of the Lord!

 Question for us: Does it make you happy to know God's salvation? Why?

 Knowing God better: God always keeps His promises. Although his people often rebelled, He always remained the one who patiently expected repentance, and who always remained faithful to everything He had promised for them.

GOD IS UNCONDITIONALLY FAITHFUL..

 Main characters
Zephaniah: Prophet and great-great-grandson of a king.

 Recommendation of verse to memorize:

Zephaniah 3:17-18a
The Lord your God is with you, the Mighty Warrior who saves.
He will take great delight in you; in his love he will no longer rebuke you, but will rejoice over you with singing."

What other verses would you add?

_____   _____
_____   _____
_____   _____

Download the "Family Readings and Conversations" from:
www.e625.com/lessons

78

Lesson 20 > ESTHER

General information about the book
The book about the queen who served God. This book and Ruth are the only books named after women.
It has 10 chapters.

Who wrote it and in what era?
The author is unknown, although Mordecai, Ezra or Nehemiah may be options. It was written around the year 400 B.C.

Purpose of the book
The book tells us about the liberation of the Jews. The modern descendants of the Jews read this book during the feast of Purim in memory of that liberation. It shows us how God cares for his children. Even we do not fully know God's plan for us, we are sure it's a good one.

Introductory activity
Kings and Queens
Using sheets of paper we will make crowns for kings and queens. The crowns should be decorated in the most creative ways possible.

Let's connect: God calls us a people of kings and priests. To be kings or queens we must behave properly before God and understand that if we are given authority it is not for our own benefit, but to serve others.

Initial discussion:
How many countries have kings today? What did kings do in ancient times?

What do we learn about God in this book?

This is why God brought you
God allowed Esther to become queen during the time of King Ahasuerus. Esther had a cousin named Mordecai, who advised her on how to become queen. Morde-cai learned of a conspiracy that two men were planning to kill the king. Mordecai told the king what they were up to, saving his life. Although the fact was recorded in the palace books, Mordecai was never rewarded.

This king had a second in command called Amman. He hated the Jews, and asked the king to allow him to exterminate them. The king, without understanding the situation, gave him permission. Mordecai, upon learning about this, told Queen Esther to speak to the king to save her people, saying: "Who knows if you were not brought to the throne precisely for a time like this!"

As Haman prepared the gallows to kill Mordecai, the king decided to review the history of his kingdom, and when he saw the story where Mordecai had saved him from those two evildoers who wanted to harm him, he asked, "How did we reward Mordecai for such an act? At that moment he realized that they had never rewarded him. Haman was arriving at that time and the king asked: "What do you think would be a suitable reward for someone whom the king wishes to honor?" Haman, thinking he was talking about him, said: "Dress him in the king's mantle, let him ride one of his horses and proclaim it loudly so that everyone can hear it."

Then the king told Haman to do what he had just described to Mordecai. Haman was enraged, but Mordecai was treated as Haman said. The Jews were saved and Haman was punished.

 Question for us: What do you think is the moral of this story?

 Knowing God better: God has a plan for your life. That plan is good, and He wants to use you to bless many. Do good no matter who it's for. Don't let envy divert you from God's plan for you. God made you special, he made you good for many things and not so good for others. Understand that God wants to use all that he gave you.

GOD IS IN CONTROL.

 Main characters
Esther: replaced Vashti as queen of Persia.
Mordecai: adopted and raised Esther; advised her when she was queen and eventually replaced Haman as second in command of King Xerxes' kingdom.
King Xerxes: king of Persia who married Esther.
Haman: second in command of king Xerxes; tried to kill all the Jews.

Recommendation of verse to memorize:

Esther 4:14b

And who knows but that you have come to your royal position for such a time as this?

What other verses would you add?

_____   _____
_____   _____
_____   _____

**Download the "Family Readings and Conversations" from:
www.e625.com/lessons**

Lesson 21 > NEHEMIAH

General information about the book
Nehemiah is the book that tells us about the reconstruction of the walls. It has 13 chapters.

Who wrote it and in what era?
Although much of the book was taken from Nehemiah's personal notes, Ezra is recognized as the author of this book.

Purpose of the book
This is the last of the historical books of the Old Testament. The book shows us Nehemiah's leadership in the reconstruction of the city, as he gave up a comfortable life as the king's cupbearer.

Introductory activity
Walls
With sheets of paper we will make the largest walls we can make. The tallest wall will win.

Let's connect: We will learn about the life of Nehemiah, who he had to rebuild his city's walls.

Initial discussion:
Why do you think the walls were important in ancient cities? How do you imagine them?

What do we learn about God in this book?

Willing to change his life
Nehemiah was the king's cupbearer. That means that he was the one who brought drinks to the king. In ancient times, that position was very well paid and held in high regard. Nehemiah lived a very comfortable life.

One day he received news from his brother Hanani, that the walls of Jerusalem were still in ruins; and Nehemiah wept with pain and could not eat anymore. He begged the Lord to allow him to go to help rebuild the walls, and asked Him to forgive his people for all the evil they had done.

When the king saw that Nehemiah was sad, he gave him permission to go, and also gave him money and materials to build the wall.

 Question for us: Have you ever given up something you really liked in order to help others?

 Knowing God better: Nehemiah did not think only about his own welfare, but instead he thought about how to help his brothers. God rewarded him with the favor of the king, who not only gave him permission to build the wall, but also helped him with the materials. God helps you when you desire to help others.

GOD IS A PROVIDER.

Repairing the walls

Nehemiah arrived to rebuild the walls, and soon organized everyone to work. He really was a great leader.

Seeing that they were making progress, two Samaritans called Sanballat and Tobiah conspired to kill Nehemiah, and began mocking the work building the walls. Then Nehemiah told the workers to carry weapons with them, to be prepared, but not to stop working.

They finished the reconstruction of the wall in 52 days, and when they finished even their enemies were afraid, because they realized that God was with them.

 Question for us: What do you do when someone makes fun of a job you are doing?

 Knowing God better: Nehemiah was not intimidated or frightened by people who mocked the work they were doing. Everyone was telling them that it was impossible to get it done, and that it was going to look bad. Nehemiah trusted God and did not listen to the mockery. The result was that they finished the reconstruction in RECORD time.

GOD IS POWERFUL.

 Main characters
Nehemiah: the cupbearer of King Artaxerxes.
Ezra: leader of the second group of exiles.
Samballat and Tobiah: they mocked those who were rebuilding the walls.

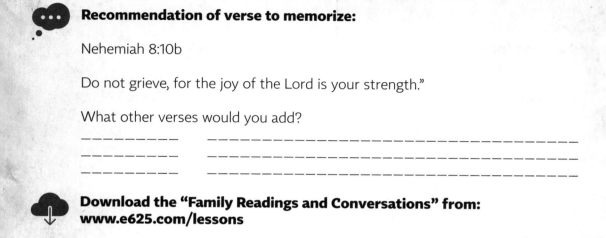

Recommendation of verse to memorize:

Nehemiah 8:10b

Do not grieve, for the joy of the Lord is your strength."

What other verses would you add?

_____   _____
_____   _____
_____   _____

Download the "Family Readings and Conversations" from:
www.e625.com/lessons

Lesson 22 > HAGGAI

General information about the book

He was the first prophet who spoke after the return of the people from Babylon. The book is one of the three books of the prophets who prophesied after the exile. It has 2 chapters.

Who wrote it and in what era?

It was the year 520 BC. and during this time the Persian kings were still dominant. Haggai was sent by God to speak to the people. We don't know much about him, but he is described as a messenger or angel from God. Fortunately, the people paid attention to his words.

Purpose of the book

Haggai's main concern was the rebuilding of the temple. The people had started to rebuild it, but then they became discouraged and abandoned it for fifteen long years. Apparently they forgot about God for a long time! Haggai got their attention and at the same time encouraged them to be faithful to God and complete their task.

Introductory activity

Let's form teams of four people. We will give each person separate instructions. We will tell two of them that they have to express appreciation, affection, affirmation to one of the other two people. Mainly it will be verbal. They will congratulate them on positive things, or give them compliments. We will tell the other two people that, while being respectful, they should ignore, avoid, and not listen to the people who speak to them. They can become distracted, talk to each other, turn around, etc., to ignore those who are trying to say something positive.

Let's connect: They can note how easy it is to become distracted from what is important, and above all how easy it is to ignore others. They can also feel how annoying it is to be ignored. This is very similar to what was happening between the people and God Himself.

Initial discussion:

Why do you think God's people was willing to ignore God? Do you think God liked it? Do you think that despite this God still loved them?

What do we learn about God in this book?

(Haggai 1:1-5)

To God's people, the temple represented God's presence. It also was a symbol that announced to other peoples who the true God was. When the Jews returned from exile they began the construction of the temple, but then they became demotivated and abandoned this important work. Instead of being concerned about honoring God, they dedicated themselves to building their own luxurious houses and became more interested in their own prestige. It is not that they thought that God was not important, just that He was not as important. In fact, it seems that for them obedience was something that began with the word "later."

Question for us: How important is it to you to obey God? Do you choose to obey now, today, or leave it for later, another day?

Knowing God better: God expects us to honor him as our God, and this means that there is nothing and no one more important than Him. When He asks us to obey it is always for the best and we must always comply without waiting.

GOD IS WORTHY OF OUR OBEDIENCE.

(Haggai 1:6-11)

Hoping that the people would understand their spiritual problems, God used a strategy to attract their attention: He caused a drought. It had not rained, and the harvest was poor. The people didn't have food, and they were tired of working so hard for such a small harvest. Sadly, they thought this was something normal, or natural, simple bad luck. However, God affirmed that He was the one who had brought the drought. God never seeks revenge, and doesn't want to hurt us; He wants us to learn about our mistakes and to genuinely repent. Sometimes He has to use what we may call punishment, to get us to react.

Question for us: Has God ever used something painful to get you to realize that you were not obeying Him? Isn't it better to obey before any punishment comes?

Knowing God better: God will never abandon us, even if we ignore Him or avoid Him; But disobedience never brings a blessing. He always gives us a new opportunity to repent and return to Him

GOD IS MERCIFUL AND PATIENT.

(Haggai 1:12-15)

The leaders, and then all the people listened to the voice of God through Haggai. Great news! They recognized their sin and decided to obey. For God the important thing was not the construction of a building, but the heart of his people: They recognized Him as their God and served Him instead of serving themselves. History tells us that it took them four years to rebuild the entire temple.

 Question for us: Have you ever obeyed "on the outside", but were unwilling to obey "on the inside"? How should our obedience to God be?

 Knowing God better: God closely watches our actions, but he is the only one who can also truly see our heart. The appearance of obedience may deceive others, but it does not deceive God. This is good news! He can see our inner self and tells us what we must change to avoid contaminating our heart with disobedience.

GOD IS PERFECTLY HOLY.

 Main characters
Haggai: prophet sent by God to challenge and encourage the people.
Zerubbabel: the governor, the political leader of the people.
Joshua: the high priest, the religious leader of the people.

 Recommendation of verse to memorize:

Haggai 1:13

Then Haggai, the Lord's messenger, gave this message of the Lord to the people: "I am with you," declares the Lord.

What other verses would you add?

_____ _____
_____ _____
_____ _____

 Download the "Family Readings and Conversations" from:
www.e625.com/lessons

Lesson 23 > MALACHI

General information about the book
Malachi represents the last prophetic words of the Old Testament.
It has 4 chapters.

Who wrote it and in what era?
The book is believed to be anonymous because the name of the book means "my messenger." It was written at the end of the fifth century B.C.

Purpose of the book:
Malachi represents the latest of the times of the Old Testament prophets. He rebuked the people for their sins, and also predicted the coming of Jesus.

Introductory activity:
Do you know who I am?
In pairs, we will put the name of a famous TV celebrity on the back of one of the partners. He will have to guess who it is. He can only ask questions that can only be answered with "yes" or "no".

Let's connect: If we know a persons characteristics, their behavior, what they do, etc., we can describe them. Often we don't know how God behaves, because we don't know Him well. We need to learn to know Him.

Initial discussion:
What do you know about how God behaves, and about who He is?

What do we learn about God in this book?

(Malachi 2:13-14)
And they still ask why.
In the book of Malachi, God scolds the people of Israel. The people of Israel complain that God does not help them, but God tells them the they should not be surprised that bad things happen to them, if they have turned away from God.

Question for us: Can you remember a punishment that your parents gave you for misbehaving?

Knowing God better: The people of Israel were behaving badly, and yet they were asking God why he didn't bless them. We must always seek to please God.

GOD REWARDS.

(Malachi 4:1-2)

God promised to reward those who act with righteousness and seek to please God. Although at times it seems that those who do bad things receive no consequences, and even do well, God has said that justice will be done and that His light will shine on those who do good, and they will rejoice like a newly fed calf. So, we will be very happy!

 Question for us: Have you ever seen someone who did done something wrong, and was not punished?

 Knowing God better: Even when we see that doing evil is not being punished, we must be firm in doing good ... at the end, God will reward our works.

GOD IS MERCIFUL AND JUST.

 Main characters
Malachi: last of the Old Testament prophets.

 Recommendation of verse to memorize:
Malachi 4:2
But for you who revere my name, the sun of righteousness will rise with healing in its rays. And you will go out and frolic like well-fed calves.

What other verses would you add?

_ _ _ _ _ _ _ _ _   _
_ _ _ _ _ _ _ _ _   _
_ _ _ _ _ _ _ _ _   _

 Download the "Family Readings and Conversations" from:
www.e625.com/lessons

NEW TESTAMENT

The whole **BIBLE** *in a year*
⟶ FOR ⟵
CHILDREN

Lesson 24 > THE GOSPELS (part one)

The incarnation of Christ
General information about the book
The gospels narrate the life and works of Jesus Christ.
There are four gospels: Matthew, Mark, Luke and John.
Matthew has 28 chapters, Mark 16, Luke 24 and John 21.

Who wrote it and in what era?
Matthew wrote the gospel that bears his name; Mark is said to have been the writer for the apostle Peter, while Luke is said to have been Paul's writing partner. John wrote the gospel that bears his name.
The gospels were written after the death of Jesus and before the year 100 A.D.

Purpose of the book
The purpose of the gospels is to present Jesus as the Messiah and tell us his story and his works. The focus of Matthew's gospel is the Jews, while Mark may have focused on those who were not Jews. Luke presents Jesus closer to men, while John emphasizes the love of God and Jesus as the Son of God.

Introductory activity
The Christmas story
Let's put in a bowl the names of Joseph, Mary, shepherds (as many as necessary), Angel Gabriel, the Eastern kings, and the animals of the stable. We distribute the papers and we recreate the Christmas story.

Let's read:
Mary and the angel Gabriel: Luke 1: 26-38.
Birth of Jesus Luke 2: 8-20.
Sages from the East: Matthew 2: 1-2 and 2: 10-11.

Let's connect: Jesus is our great gift. Jesus came into the world and became a man born through Mary who had never been married. He became a man to save us and to die for our sins.

Initial discussion:
Why do you think we give gifts at Christmas?

What do we learn about God in this book?

In the beginning was the word

At the beginning of his Gospel, John wrote the following statement:

> 1 In the beginning was the Word, and the Word was with God, and the Word was God.
> 2 He was with God in the beginning.
> 3 Through him all things were made; without him nothing was made that has been made.
> 4 In him was life, and that life was the light of all mankind.
> 5 The light shines in the darkness, and the darkness has not overcome it.

John tells us that Jesus, being God, became man and lived among us. Jesus is God. Seeing that no one could save us, God decided to send his son to save us.

 Question for us: What is the word? What words do you know?

 Knowing God better: John says that Jesus is the Word. We preach Jesus when we put into practice the Word of God, not when we just read it or tell it. The word represents action. Running, laughing, loving, living, forgiving, are words. If we don't put them into practice, we are not preaching Jesus who is the Word. God wants us to know His Word, but He wants us even more to put into practice His Word.

JESUS IS GOD.

 Main characters
Jesus: our Savior and the Son of God.
Joseph: the earthly father of Jesus.
Mary: the earthly mother of Jesus.
The wise men: they brought gifts to Jesus.
The angel Gabriel: the messenger sent by God to announce to Mary that she will be the mother of Jesus.

Recommendation of verse to memorize:

Matthew 1:23

"The virgin will conceive and give birth to a son, and they will call him Immanuel" (which means "God with us").

What other verses would you add?

_____   _____
_____   _____
_____   _____

Download the "Family Readings and Conversations" from: www.e625.com/lessons

Lesson 25 > THE GOSPELS (part two)

The ministry of Jesus
General information about the book
The gospels narrate the life and works of Jesus Christ.
There are four gospels: Matthew, Mark, Luke and John.
Matthew has 28 chapters, Mark 16, Luke 24 and John 21.

Who wrote it and in what era?
Matthew wrote the gospel that bears his name; Mark is said to have been the writer for the apostle Peter, while Luke is said to have been Paul's writing partner. John wrote the gospel that bears his name.
The gospels were written after the death of Jesus and before the year 100 A.D.

Purpose of the book
The purpose of the gospels is to present Jesus as the Messiah and tell us his story and his works. The focus of Matthew's gospel is the Jews, while Mark may have focused on those who were not Jews. Luke presents Jesus closer to men, while John emphasizes the love of God and Jesus as the Son of God.

Introductory activity
The race of the needy
We will race trying to carry one of our friends from one point of the room to another without walking.
Upon reaching the marked point we will blindfold him and return to the starting point by surrounding him and only guiding it with our voices. If our friend who is blindfolded touches one of the other friends or bumps into something, he must return and start again. The team that arrives first to the original starting point wins.

Let's connect: During his stay on earth Jesus performed many miracles, giving sight to the blind, making the lame walk, etc. Jesus did lots of good works and amazing things during his ministry. Today we will study that.

Initial discussion:
What miracles from Jesus do you remember?

What do we learn about God in this book?

Calling the disciples - Mark 1: 14-20

Jesus walked through his city, looking for people to call to follow Him. For example, Jesus watched Simon and Andrew throwing their nets into the waters of the sea of Galilee and said, "Come and follow me." He told them that instead of fishing they could fish people for God. Then he kept walking and saw James and his brother John who were repairing their fishing nets. He also told them the same thing, "Come and follow me." They left their boat and left with Jesus. That's how Jesus started calling each one of those who would become his beloved disciples.

 Question for us: Have you ever had to stop doing something you liked to be able to obey (for example your parents)?

Knowing God better: Simon and Andrew, John and James, and the other disciples were busy doing what they liked to do, but Jesus asked them to follow Him. Sometimes our parents interrupt us while we are doing something we like to do, to ask as to do something else. For example, they may ask us to stop playing and come into the house to clean up our room. To obey the call of our parents can be compared to obeying Jesus when he called his disciples.

JESUS CHOOSES US.

Miracles of Jesus

Luke 1:37 says, "Nothing is impossible for God."
Jesus performed many miracles while walking on earth, showing that nothing is impossible for God.
Some of his miracles were:
> Turned water into wine at a party (John 2: 1-11).
> Healed Peter's mother-in-law (Matthew 8: 14-17).
> Healed a paralytic (Matthew 9: 1-8 or Mark 2: 1-12 or Luke 5: 17-26).
> Resurrected a widow's son (Luke 7: 11-17).
> Gave sight to a blind man (Matthew 9: 27-31),
> Fed five thousand people with only five loaves and two fish (Matthew 14: 13-21).
> Healed a deaf mute (Mark 7: 31-37).

Reading about the miracles of Jesus fills us with a powerful emotion, and the confidence that we have a powerful God for whom nothing is impossible.

 Question for us: Do you remember a situation in which you asked Jesus to help you with something difficult for you or your family? Have you been sick and prayed to God?

 Knowing God better: God is the same yesterday, today and forever. His power is enormous and there is nothing impossible for Him. When you read about each of Jesus' miracles, you see that He was first asked for help, and then He did the miracle. Jesus can hear you when you have a need. His power remains endless and He continues to work miracles in our lives.

JESUS IS MIRACULOUS.

 Main characters
Jesus: our Savior and the Son of God.
Simon, Andrew, James, John: fishermen who followed Jesus and became His disciples.

 Recommendation of verse to memorize:

Luke 1:37

For with God nothing shall be impossible.

What other verses would you add?

_____   _____
_____   _____
_____   _____

 Download the "Family Readings and Conversations" from:
www.e625.com/lessons

Lesson 26 > THE GOSPELS (part three)

The teachings of Jesus
General information about the book
The gospels narrate the life and works of Jesus Christ.
There are four gospels: Matthew, Mark, Luke and John.
Matthew has 28 chapters, Mark 16, Luke 24 and John 21.

Who wrote it and in what era?
Matthew wrote the gospel that bears his name; Mark is said to have been the writer for the apostle Peter, while Luke is said to have been Paul's writing partner. John wrote the gospel that bears his name.
The gospels were written after the death of Jesus and before the year 100 A.D.

Purpose of the book
The purpose of the gospels is to present Jesus as the Messiah and tell us his story and his works. The focus of Matthew's gospel is the Jews, while Mark may have focused on those who were not Jews. Luke presents Jesus closer to men, while John emphasizes the love of God and Jesus as the Son of God.

Introductory activity
Hide-and-seek
It is the classic version of hide-and-seek, in which a person covers his eyes, counts to twenty, and then goes to find the other players. The difficulty of the game is that both those who hide and the one who seeks will be blindfolded.

Let's connect: Jesus taught many things during his ministry, and one of them was to go pray in a secluded or hidden place, so that other people do not see you pray, allowing your prayer to be only for God.

Initial discussion:
Where in your house can you pray?

What do we learn about God in this book?

Teaching us how to pray - Matthew 6: 9-15

Jesus taught us how to pray: We should not be like those who want everyone to see them praying. Prayer should be something private, where we thank God, we praise him, we ask him to help us and we tell him that we will try to do what's right. When you pray to God you must communicate from your heart, talk about how you feel, and not repeat things just to repeat them. When you have a need, pray. When you're grateful, pray. When you're sad, pray. When you're happy, pray. Pray whenever you can to God. Prayer is your communication with God.

 Question for us: How is your prayer to God?

 Knowing God better: Prayer is a conversation, and Jesus taught us that it must come from the heart, and it should be only between you and Him.

JESUS TEACHES US.

Love your enemies - Matthew 6: 43-48

When we get angry with someone, we usually want to treat him badly. Jesus taught many things that were different from what normally happens. For example, he told us that if we loved or treated well only those who treat us well, we have no merit. Jesus said that if someone was our enemy we should love him and pray for him. He also said that if someone wanted to be the first or the leader, he should serve others. Thinking as Jesus teaches us makes us different, because his teachings are wiser.

 Question for us: Can you think of someone you should forgive because he recently made you angry or hurt you?

 Knowing God better: We can pray for those people who have hurt us or have made us angry, and say that we forgive them.

JESUS FORGIVES US.

Main characters

Jesus: our Savior and the Son of God.
Disciples: those who decide to follow Jesus.

Recommendation of verse to memorize:

Matthew 5: 9
Blessed are the peacemakers, for they will be called children of God.

What other verses would you add?

_____   _____
_____   _____
_____   _____

Download the "Family Readings and Conversations" from:
www.e625.com/lessons

Lesson 27 > THE GOSPELS (part four)

Parables

General information about the book
The gospels narrate the life and works of Jesus Christ.
There are four gospels: Matthew, Mark, Luke and John.
Matthew has 28 chapters, Mark 16, Luke 24 and John 21.

Who wrote it and in what era?
Matthew wrote the gospel that bears his name; Mark is said to have been the writer for the apostle Peter, while Luke is said to have been Paul's writing partner. John wrote the gospel that bears his name.
The gospels were written after the death of Jesus and before the year 100 A.D.

Purpose of the book
The purpose of the gospels is to present Jesus as the Messiah and tell us his story and his works. The focus of Matthew's gospel is the Jews, while Mark may have focused on those who were not Jews. Luke presents Jesus closer to men, while John emphasizes the love of God and Jesus as the Son of God.

Introductory activity:
Riddles
Divided into teams, we'll select five riddles per team, and we'll have a contest to see who solves the most.

Let's connect: Jesus spoke to the Pharisees in parables because he wanted his disciples to understand Him while making it difficult for the Pharisees. A parable is a fictional story that illustrates a truth.

Initial discussion:
What parables of Jesus have you heard?

What do we learn about God in this book?

The kingdom of heaven Matthew 13: 31-32
Jesus compared the kingdom of heaven to several things. One of those things was a mustard seed. A mustard tree is large and strong but its seed is very small.

Jesus said: "The kingdom of heaven is like a mustard seed, that a man sowed in his field. Although it is the smallest of all the seeds, when it grows it is the largest of the vegetables and becomes a tree, so that the birds come and nest in its branches."

Question for us: Are you familiar with the seeds of any fruit, and do you know what their tree looks like?

Knowing God better: The kingdom of heaven is like a mustard seed, because it starts to germinate in our hearts with very small teachings, but it grows and grows until it becomes big in us.

JESUS IS CREATIVE.

Parable of the Good Samaritan - Luke 10: 25-37

Let's read the story of the good Samaritan. This story Jesus used to explain who he meant when he was talking about loving others. Here we can see that Jesus says that our neighbor is the one who is near us and has a need.

Question for us: Who have you helped lately that had a need?

Knowing God better: Jesus says that the law can be summed up in loving God with all our strength, mind and heart and our neighbor as ourselves. When we help someone in need we are helping our neighbor and fulfilling God's law.

JESUS IS LOVE.

Parable of the prodigal son - Luke 15: 11-31

Let's read the story of the prodigal son. In this parable Jesus teaches us that behaving badly against our parents or against God brings us consequences, but in spite of everything, if we decide to repent, God will always be ready to receive us.

Question for us: Has something bad ever happened to you because you disobeyed?

Knowing God better: If we disobey we will surely have consequences, not because God is evil, but because He wants us to learn. But God will always be there waiting for us with open arms to forgive us, if we repent.

GOD IS OUR FATHER.

 Main characters
Jesus: our Savior and the Son of God.

 Recommendation of verse to memorize:

Luke 10:36-37
"Which of these three do you think was a neighbor to the man who fell into the hands of robbers?"
The expert in the law replied,
　　"The one who had mercy on him."
Jesus told him,
　　"Go and do likewise."

What other verses would you add?
_____　_____
_____　_____
_____　_____

 Download the "Family Readings and Conversations" from:
　www.e625.com/lessons

Lesson 28 > THE GOSPELS *(part five)*

Arrest, death, resurrection and appearance of Jesus
General information about the book
The gospels narrate the life and works of Jesus Christ.
There are four gospels: Matthew, Mark, Luke and John.
Matthew has 28 chapters, Mark 16, Luke 24 and John 21.

Who wrote it and in what era?
Matthew wrote the gospel that bears his name; Mark is said to have been the writer for the apostle Peter, while Luke is said to have been Paul's writing partner. John wrote the gospel that bears his name.
The gospels were written after the death of Jesus and before the year 100 A.D.

Purpose of the book
The purpose of the gospels is to present Jesus as the Messiah and tell us his story and his works. The focus of Matthew's gospel is the Jews, while Mark may have focused on those who were not Jews. Luke presents Jesus closer to men, while John emphasizes the love of God and Jesus as the Son of God.

Introductory activity
Carrying logs
Pick up a log or a heavyweight and try to carry it any way you can from one point to another; Then someone else will relieve you and take your load to return. This game is played in teams, and the team that finishes the established route first wins.

Let's connect: Jesus carried the cross on his way to Mount Golgotha, where they crucified him; At some point he fell, and a bystander helped him carry it.

Initial discussion:
Have you ever helped a friend, or have you ever been helped, after a hard stumble or fall?

What do we learn about God in this book?

The Last Supper - John 13

Jesus knew that the time for Him to return to the Father was close. He decided to sit down for dinner with his disciples and accomplished several things with them. First, He taught them that if they wanted to be part of His kingdom they should serve each other. To show them, he washed their feet, as a sign that if He, being who He was, washed their feet (which was something only servants did), they should also serve each other without problems.

Then he taught them that they should love each other with a love as strong as the love He had for them. Jesus wanted the world to recognize that they were his disciples because of the strong love they had for each other.

He also told them that he no longer called them servants. Now he called them friends. And that friends are those who love each other very much and take care of each other.

 Question for us: What kind of service would you be willing to do for your friends?

[↑] Knowing God better: The strongest teaching that Jesus gave us in this passage is the love that those who follow Jesus should have for one another. The world will know that we are His children because of how we love each other, and so they will believe in God.

JESUS IS OUR FRIEND.

The crucifixion - John 19: 17-37

Judas, who was one of Jesus' friends, betrayed him and sold him for money to those who wanted to kill him. Instead of showing anger, Jesus surrendered. Peter did not want Him to be taken away, but Jesus did not resist.

Jesus was brought before the High Priest and before the Roman governor. He carried a cross on his shoulders with which they would crucify him.

The Roman governor told the people to choose between freeing a murderer and crucifying Jesus. They chose to free the murderer. Thus, Jesus was taken, nailed to the cross, and crucified, until he died.

As he was dyeing, Jesus asked the Father to forgive them, because they did not know what they were doing. When he died there was an earthquake and the sky became dark.

They lowered His body from the cross and took it to the grave where it would stay, according to them.

 Question for us: Would you like to receive Jesus as your Lord and Savior, and give thanks for His forgiveness of your sins and for HIs sacrifice at the cross?

 Knowing God better: Jesus died on the cross in order to pay for our sins. In the Old Testament, when forgiveness was being asked for sins a lamb was sacrificed. Jesus is the lamb of God who was sacrificed and suffered so that you and I could be forgiven of our sins. What a great love God had, who sent his only son to die for us! He who believes in Him will have eternal life.

JESUS IS THE LAMB THAT REMOVES THE SINS OF THE WORLD.

The Resurrection - John 20: 1-18

Mary Magdalene wanted to anoint Jesus' body so she went to the grave early in the morning. And what was her surprise? The grave was empty! Jesus had risen! Jesus died for our sins but He did not stay there; He rose again and now He reigns with power at the right hand of God the Father.

Jesus asked Mary: "Why do you seek the living among the dead?" Mary ran desperately to tell the disciples and told them: "He is no longer dead! He is alive!". Today we can celebrate that Jesus lives!

 Question for us: How would you have reacted if you had found the tomb empty?

 Knowing God better: We rejoice because Jesus gave himself up and died for our sins, but he did not remain dead. He rose and He lives today. What a joy it is for us to know that we can talk to a living God!

GOD IS OUR FATHER.

 Main characters
Jesús: our savior and the Son of God.
María Magdalena: found the empty tomb.

Recommendation of verse to memorize:

John 10:11
I am the good shepherd. The good shepherd lays down his life for the sheep.

What other verses would you add?

————————   ———————————————————————————————
————————   ———————————————————————————————
————————   ———————————————————————————————

 Download the "Family Readings and Conversations" from:
www.e625.com/lessons

Lesson 29 > ACTS (part one)

Chapters 1 to 6

General information about the book
This is the book that tells us the actions of the apostles.
It has 28 chapters.

Who wrote it and in what era?
Although the author is not identified, it is believed that it was Luke. Possibly Paul helped him write it. The book describes events starting on the year 33 A.D.

Purpose of the book
It presents the works of the apostles after the resurrection of Jesus. It starts by telling us what happened right after the resurrection; It tells us how the gift of the Holy Spirit was given to those who believed, and narrates the ministry of the apostles.

Introductory activity
Several tongues
We will learn to say John 3:16 in five languages:
Dio ha tanto amato il mondo da dare il suo unico Figlio perché chi crede in lui non muoia ma abbia vita eterna.
Porque Deus tanto amou o mundo que deu o seu Filho Unigênito, para que todo o que nele crer não pereça, mas tenha a vida eterna.
Porque de tal manera amó Dios al mundo, que ha dado a su Hijo unigénito, para que todo aquel que en él cree, no se pierda, mas tenga vida eterna.
Car Dieu a tellement aimé le monde qu'il a donné son Fils unique, afin que quiconque croit en lui ne soit pas perdu mais qu'il ait la vie éternelle.
Denn so hat Gott der Welt seine Liebe gezeigt: Er gab seinen einzigen Sohn dafür, dass jeder, der an ihn glaubt, nicht ins Verderben geht, sondern ewiges Leben hat.

Can you identify what language each verse is in?

Let's connect: One of the first manifestations of the Holy Spirit in the book of Acts is that as Peter preached, everyone understood the message, even though they all spoke different languages. It was like having a translator available for each language. Imagine how amazing that would be!

Initial discussion:
How do you say "son" in each of those languages?

 What do we learn about God in this book?

The power of the Holy Spirit - Acts 2: 1-47

The disciples were together in a room in Jerusalem, waiting for God to tell them what to do. In Jerusalem there were people from all over the world; They had arrived for the Feast of Pentecost.

Suddenly, a sound like a strong wind blew into the house, filling it with noise. Something like flames seemed to burn in the air and touched every person who was there. As the Holy Spirit touched them, they all started speaking in other languages.

The people thought the disciples were drunk; Then Peter spoke, and started to preach about Jesus to a great crowd. That day more than three thousand people became followers of Jesus.

 Question for us: Do you want to ask the Lord for the Holy Spirit?

 Knowing God better: Jesus made them a promise, and they waited for the promise. Suddenly, they were filled with the Holy Spirit. To everyone who asks the Lord for the Spirit, He will give it.

THE HOLY SPIRIT IS GOD.

Peter, John, and the paralytic

One afternoon, when John and Peter went to pray to the temple, they met a man asking for alms. They stopped, and the man thought they were going to give him money. Peter and John told him: "I don't have gold or silver, but I will give you what I have. In the name of Jesus, get up and go! "

That man had not been able to walk for over 40 hears, and instantly he entered the temple walking and praising God. People were amazed and scared.

 Question for us: Whom have you helped, despite not being able to give him money?

Knowing God better: The Lord left us the Holy Spirit so we can help others, and not all problems can be solved with money. It is more powerful to pray for people and let God work in their life.

GOD IS POWERFUL.

 Main characters
Peter and John: apostles of Jesus.
Paralytic: he had been paralyzed for 40 years and was healed.

 Recommendation of verse to memorize:

Acts 4:12
Salvation is found in no one else, for there is no other name under heaven given to mankind by which we must be saved.

What other verses would you add?
_____   _____
_____   _____
_____   _____

 Download the "Family Readings and Conversations" from:
www.e625.com/lessons

Lesson 30 > ACTS (part two)

Chapters from 7 to 12

General information about the book
This is the book that tells us the actions of the apostles.
It has 28 chapters.

Who wrote it and in what era?
Although the author is not identified, it is believed that it was Luke. Possibly Paul helped him write it. The book describes events starting on the year 33 A.D.

Purpose of the book
It presents the works of the apostles after the resurrection of Jesus. It starts by telling us what happened right after the resurrection; It tells us how the gift of the Holy Spirit was given to those who believed, and narrates the ministry of the apostles.

Introductory activity
One of the players, chosen at random, stands with his back to the group, and hands against a wall. When the order is given he can start chasing the others. When he touches someone he says "trapped" and they both go to the wall, turn their backs to the group, hold each others hands, and then start chasing others, and this continues until everyone is caught. When, for whatever reason, they stop holding hands, the others can hit them on the back.

Let's connect: Today we played a chasing game, but during the time of the apostles they were the ones being chased and persecuted, and it was not very nice for them. They knew that they were serving and pleasing God, even though others were persecuting them. Today we are going to study the section of the book of Acts that tells us how the apostles were being persecuted.

Initial discussion:
How do you think it feels to be persecuted?

What do we learn about God in this book?

Perseguidos - Hechos 6:1-7:60
After the paralytic was healed, Peter and John were captured and taken to the priests, who wanted to see by whose power they had done that. They did not

understand what was happening. They put them in jail, but at night an angel came to the jail, opened the doors and led them out. The angel told them to go to the temple and share the good news.

Some began to persecute them for preaching Jesus. A sage named Gamaliel told those who were persecuting them to leave them alone, because if this was from God, then no one would be able to stop them. Indeed, to this day no one has been able to stop us from preaching Jesus!

A man named Saul (who would later become the apostle Paul), had another disciple of Jesus named Stephen stoned and killed. While they were stoning him, Stephen prayed to God to forgive them, because they did not know what they were doing. Stephen was received in heaven as a hero!

 Question for us: Have you ever been harassed for being a follower of Jesus?

 Knowing God better: Many people do not understand what it means to be a follower of Jesus. When someone harasses you for doing what Jesus told us to do, remember that even the apostles were persecuted for doing what Jesus commanded, but the power of God will always be shown in your life.

GOD TESTIFIES ABOUT US.

From Saul to Paul - Acts 9

Saul was a well educated person who persecuted those who believed in Jesus in order to kill them. He hated them and wanted to destroy them.

On one of Saul's trips to persecute believers, a bright light from the heavens suddenly appeared and threw him off his horse. Saul, blinded by the light, only heard a voice that said: "Saul, Saul, why do you persecute me?" Saul asked who he was and Jesus said: "I am Jesus, whom you are persecuting." Then Jesus ordered him to go to a city called Damascus. There a man named Ananias prayed for him to recover his sight.

Saul had converted, and was now a follower of Jesus. From then on they called him Paul. The Christians were afraid of him at first because they did not know if his conversion was real, but Paul kept preaching Jesus wherever he went.

Question for us: Do you think Jesus can change even the most wicked? Do you know someone whom Jesus has changed?

 Knowing God better: Jesus changed Paul, who had done lots of evil to the church, and He not only changed him: He made him a preacher of his gospel.

For God there is no one so evil that He cannot change him.

GOD CHANGES LIVES..

 Main characters

Gamaliel: Wise man who said that the disciples shouldn't be harassed anymore.
Stephen: obedient disciple who died while preaching Jesus.
Saul: persecutor of the church.
Paul: the name of Saul after he accepted Jesus.

 Recommendation of verse to memorize:

Acts 10:35
But in every nation whoever fears Him and works righteousness is accepted by Him.

What other verses would you add?

_____   _____
_____   _____
_____   _____

 Download the "Family Readings and Conversations" from:
www.e625.com/lessons

Lesson 31 > ACTS (part three)

Chapters from 13 to 28

General information about the book

This is the book that tells us the actions of the apostles.
It has 28 chapters.

Who wrote it and in what era?

Although the author is not identified, it is believed that it was Luke. Possibly Paul helped him write it. The book describes events starting on the year 33 A.D.

Purpose of the book

It presents the works of the apostles after the resurrection of Jesus. It starts by telling us what happened right after the resurrection; It tells us how the gift of the Holy Spirit was given to those who believed, and narrates the ministry of the apostles.

Introductory activity

Let's take some virtual trips. Let's get some images, printed or projected, of particular landscapes or scenes from different countries of the world. The goal is for the children to guess to which country they belong. If you prefer, do not show the complete image at first, but reveal it slowly. When they identify the country, ask them to imagine what kind of food they eat there, how their language sound (tell them to make up some words!), and what are some of their customs.

Let's connect: The apostles mobilized in different countries and cities to preach the gospel. In many places they were well received, but in others they were mistreated. However, they were always faithful to the mission entrusted to them. In every place they went, they taught others about Jesus!

Initial discussion:

Where would you like to travel? Would you be willing to go to that place to tell others about Jesus?

What do we learn about God in this book?

Paul and Silas in jail - Acts 16: 16-40

Paul and his partner Silas went everywhere preaching the gospel. Once they cast out a spirit of divination from a slave girl. The slave's masters got angry with Paul for taking away the spirit of divination, and had them put in jail.

While in the jail, Paul and Silas began to sing and pray. All the prisoners heard them, and suddenly an earthquake shook the jail. The doors opened and they were freed from their shackles. When the jailer saw that all prisoners could escape, he wanted to kill himself. But Paul stopped him, and the man asked how he could be saved. Paul replied: "Believe in the Lord Jesus Christ; and you and your family will be saved."

 Question for us: Who in your family is not a follower of Jesus?

 Knowing God better: Paul told the jailer that, if we believe, we and our family will be saved. If you believe in Jesus, you can pray to God so that your whole family will come to serve and follow Him.

GOD IS GOD OF MY FAMILY.

Paul's travels - Acts 17 to 28

Paul preached the Lord Jesus Christ everywhere he could go. He went to many cities. In some there were people who didn't even know God, so he spoke to each person the best way he could to make himself understood better.

He spoke to people who believed in God, but not in Jesus. He spoke to people who worshiped other gods. He spoke to very important people. He tried to talk to as many people as he could. God brought understanding to the people who listened to him, and many accepted Jesus as their Lord and savior.

The book of Acts seems to have no ending, because it's a book that continues to be written even today, with the acts of each one of us, as we also preach the message of Salvation.

Question for us: To which of your friends would you like to speak about Jesus?

Knowing God better: Jesus sent us to speak about Him to all the people we can. We must share God's love and goodness for us. A good way to start talking about Jesus to our friends is to tell them that God loves them, takes care of them, and will help them when they ask Him.

JESUS IS THE MESSAGE OF SALVATION..

Main characters
Paul: apostle who preached the Word to all.
Silas: Paul's partner.

Recommendation of verse to memorize:

Acts 16:31

Believe in the Lord Jesus, and you will be saved—you and your household.

What other verses would you add?

_____   _____

_____   _____

_____   _____

Download the "Family Readings and Conversations" from:
www.e625.com/lessons

Lesson 32 > JAMES

General information about the book
It talks about putting our faith into practice.
It has 5 chapters.

Who wrote it and in what era?
It was written by the apostle James, a brother of Jesus. It was written between the years 44 to 49 A.D.

Purpose of the book
This letter was written by James to tell believers in Jesus that their faith has to be accompanied by works, and that they can't just say that they believe in Jesus, but they also have to show it.

Introductory activity
James says
We are going to play a version of the game "Simon says", except that we will be saying "James says".
In the game we should all do what "James" says, but also James can say something and do something else. For example: "James says hands up" and James lowers his hands. He can also do exactly what he says.

Let's connect: People are more likely to do what they see us do, rather than what we tell them to do. That's why it is so important for us to teach others by our example.

Initial discussion:
Would you believe a person who says one thing and does the opposite?

What do we learn about God in this book?

Faith without works - James 2: 14-17

James is very clear when he tells us that if we assert that we have faith in Jesus, we must prove it. Our faith is shown by loving and helping those who need it. According to James, if we say we are Christians and we do not help those we can help, our faith is dead.
When you help someone who needs you, you are showing that you have a living faith in our Lord Jesus.

Question for us: Have you ever helped anyone?

Knowing God better: Helping those who need help shows that we truly are believers in God. For our faith to be true, we must seek to help those who we can help.

JESUS IS THE AUTHOR OF OUR FAITH.

The power of the tongue - James 3: 9-12

James says that our tongue is like the rudder of a ship, because a rudder is small and yet it can move a large ship. What size is your tongue? It is small and yet it is capable of getting you into a big mess, or of being extremely helpful. Our tongue can't be both Praising God and offending other people. That is not right. We must try to speak with goodness whenever we can.

With the tongue we praise our Lord and Father, and with it we curse human beings, who have been made in God's likeness. (3: 9).

Question for us: What do you think about curse words?

Knowing God better: The apostle James says that we should not use our mouth to say foul things and then praise God. Let's be careful about what we say, so that we can please God with our lives.

GOD LISTENS TO US.

The prayer of Faith - James 5: 13-16

The prayer of the children of God accomplishes a lot. If they have worries. They should pray. If they are happy, they should sing praises. If they are sick, they should ask others to pray for them. Prayer is powerful. God hears and answers our prayers.

Question for us: Do you need prayer for anything?

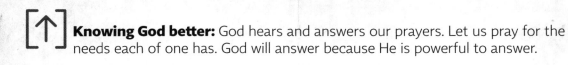

[↑] **Knowing God better:** God hears and answers our prayers. Let us pray for the needs each of one has. God will answer because He is powerful to answer.

GOD ANSWERS OUR PRAYERS.

Main characters
James: brother of Jesus and apostle.

Recommendation of verse to memorize:

James 1:19
Everyone should be quick to listen, slow to speak and slow to become angry.

What other verses would you add?
_____   _____
_____   _____
_____   _____

Download the "Family Readings and Conversations" from:
www.e625.com/lessons

Lesson 33> GALATIANS

General information about the book
Letter from the apostle Paul to the Galatians, in which he emphasizes that we are justified by faith.
The letter has 6 chapters.

Who wrote it and in what era?
It was written by the apostle Paul, most likely in the 50s AD.

Purpose of the book
Paul writes this letter to encourage and admonish the believers of the churches of Galatia. The central theme of the letter is our justification by faith.

Introductory activity
Traffic lights game
The dynamics are simple: an adult is placed at one end of the room and all minors, side by side, at the opposite end. The adult will officiate the game as the "traffic light". When he says "green light" children can move forward, but when he says "red light" they must stop. Those who continue moving forward after the order to stop will be disqualified. The player who reaches the finish line first wins ... or the only one not to be disqualified.

Let's connect: Our life is full of rules: what we are allowed to do and what we are not allowed to do. We can obey because it's a duty, or because we want to obey. God wants us to obey him because we want to do it, rather than because we must do it

Initial discussion:
What is the commandment of God that's hardest for you to obey?

What do we learn about God in this book?

Galatians 5:13-14
The apostle Paul writes the letter to the Galatians showing great concern, because after they had faithfully believed in Jesus, some people had come to try to convince them that in order to please God they had to return to practicing the rituals of the law of the Jews.

It is not that the law was bad, but Jesus' great message is that what matters to God is that we choose to do good because we love him, not because it is a duty. That is why Jesus set us free, so that we could choose to make good decisions.

 Question for us: Do we obey our parents because we must, or because we love them and want to obey them?

 Knowing God better: God likes it when we do what's good and serve him not because we have to do it but because we want to do it. What the Lord sees is our heart.

GOD GIVES US FREEDOM TO MAKE GOOD DECISIONS.

Fruit of the Spirit - Galatians 5: 22-23

How can we recognize if we are properly using the freedom that God gives us? If we use it correctly to make good decisions, we will produce good results such as having love, joy, peace, patience, gentleness, goodness, faithfulness, humility and self-control.

 Question for us: How about if each of us takes one of the characteristics of the fruit of the Spirit, and gives an example of what each of them means?

 Knowing God better: A follower of Jesus is not recognized by what he says, but because he shows the fruit of God in his life. If our parents set rules for us, it is for our own good. We should not obey them just because we have to, but we must show the fruit of the Holy Spirit when we obey them.

GOD TRANSFORMS OUR BEING.

 Main characters
Paul: apostle of Jesus who was entrusted to speak to non-Jews.
Galatians: inhabitants of the region of Galatia.

Recommendation of verse to memorize:

Galatians 6:9

Let us not become weary in doing good, for at the proper time we will reap a harvest if we do not give up.

What other verses would you add?

——————— ——————————————————————————
——————— ——————————————————————————
——————— ——————————————————————————

Download the "Family Readings and Conversations" from:
www.e625.com/lessons

Lesson 34 > 1ST AND 2ND THESSALONIANS

General information about the book
Letters from the apostle Paul to the Thessalonians, reminding us that Christ is coming again.
The first letter has 5 chapters, and the second has 3 chapters.

Who wrote it and in what era?
The apostle Paul wrote them, most likely during the 50s A.D.

Purpose of the book
Paul wrote these two letters to the Thessalonians to encourage them by reminding them of the return of the Lord Jesus Christ.

Introductory activity
El lápiz cooperativo
The shared pencil
We must tie several strings to a marker, pen or pencil (as many strings as we can fit, for example eight per pencil). Working in teams, we will write the words "will return".

Let's connect: Today we will talk about the second coming of our Lord Jesus Christ.

Initial discussion:
How do you imagine Jesus's return?

What do we learn about God in this book?

Hope after death
1 Thessalonians 4: 13-18
The apostle Paul encourages us to have hope and not be sad over those who have died. It is very hard to recover from the sadness that comes with the death of someone we loved. Paul says that those who believed in Jesus are with Him.

Jesus will return for us. Just as he left and went up to heaven, Jesus will return for us. He will come back in majesty and splendor, to the sound of God's trumpet. Then we will join those who've already died.

Question for us: From the members of your family that you met, who is already with Jesus?

 Knowing God better: Knowing that those who died before us are already with Jesus should bring us joy, because they are in a much better place than we are, and we know and trust that we will see them again.

GOD WILL RETURN FOR US.

Work - 2 Thessalonians 3: 10-13

Paul wrote to the Thessalonians to scold them very strongly, because there were people in the church who did not work, and were getting into things that they shouldn't get into. In fact, he had strong words for them: "He who does not want to work should not eat either." It is not right if, for example, at our home, we only expect to be served and we do not want to help with what we are asked to do.

 Question for us: What chores do you do to help at home?

 Knowing God better: Our work as children can be to study and get the best possible grades, and also to help clean or with house chores. Always keep an attitude of wanting to help and contribute.

GOD REWARDS WORK.

 Main characters
Paul: apostle of Jesus who was entrusted to speak to non-Jews.
Thessalonians: inhabitants of the Thessaloniki region.

 Recommendation of verse to memorize:

1st Thessalonians 5:18

Give thanks in all circumstances; for this is God's will for you in Christ Jesus.

What other verses would you add?

_____   _____
_____   _____
_____   _____

 **Download the "Family Readings and Conversations" from:
www.e625.com/lessons**

Lesson 35 > 1ST CORINTHIANS

General information about the book
Letter from the apostle Paul to the Corinthians, bringing discipline to the church.
The letter has 16 chapters.

Who wrote it and in what era?
It was written by the apostle Paul, most likely during the 50s A.D.

Purpose of the book
Paul wrote this letter to the Corinthian church to exhort them pastorally.

Introductory activity
Untie the knot
A simple and fun activity that encourages children to communicate and work
together is to have them untie a knot. You will need an even number of children
for this activity (between 8 and 12 is the ideal number). Have them stand in a circle
looking inwards. Each child puts his left hand inside the circle and grabs another
child's left hand; They do the same with their right hands. Without letting go, they
must untie themselves. The only way to achieve this is to work as a team.

Let's connect: To achieve complicated things we need several people with
different skills. The church is a body that needs different skills.

Initial discussion:
What things are you very good at?

What do we learn about God in this book?

The church as a body - 1 Corinthians 12
A body has many parts and they are all different, and have different functions.
Some parts of the body are larger, others smaller; some are visible and others
remain unseen. For example, the foot is different from the hand; The eye is different
from the heart. Because all parts of the body do their part, it works well. Just as the
body has different parts of different shapes, that is also true in the body of Christ,
which is the Church.

 Question for us: What are the body parts that you use the most when you play?

 Knowing God better: All of us are different. God made us different. We have different abilities. We must thank God for each of our abilities.

GOD IS MULTIFORM.

The most excellent path - 1 Corinthians 13

Love is the most excellent path. It is always the best path. God is love. Paul describes in this letter some of the characteristics of love:

Love is patient and kind.

Love is not envious, conceited, or proud.

It does not behave rudely, It's not selfish, Does not get angry easily, and does not hold a grudge.

It doesn't like injustices.

It forgives all mistakes, always trusts the beloved, expects the best from her and endures everything.

God's love is perfect. If we want to have a guide on how we should make our decisions, this chapter of the letter to the Corinthians could be it. Jesus' commandment is that we love one another.

 Question for us: With whom is it hard for you to express God's love lately? With whom have you been impatient, or envious, or rude or malicious?

Knowing God better: Let's always choose the path of love.

Instead of envy, let's look for goodness. Instead of rudeness, selfishness or anger, let's look for love. When we seek to love people we become more like Jesus.

GOD IS LOVE.

 Main characters

Paul: apostle of Jesus who was entrusted to speak to non-Jews.

Corinthians: inhabitants of the region of Corinth.

Recommendation of verse to memorize:

1st Corinthians 13:13

And now these three remain: faith, hope and love. But the greatest of these is love.

What other verses would you add?

_____   _____
_____   _____
_____   _____

 Download the "Family Readings and Conversations" from:
www.e625.com/lessons

Lesson 36 > 2ND CORINTIHIANS

General information about the book
Letter from the apostle Paul to the Corinthians. It contains pastoral words. The letter has 13 chapters.

Who wrote it and in what era?
It was written by the apostle Paul, most likely during the 50s A.D.

Purpose of the book
Paul wrote these two letters to the Corinthian church to rebuke them with love.

Introductory activity
My good present
Let's think of one or two people to whom we want to give a present. Using a sheet of paper folded in four and some crayons, we will make a card to give to that person or persons.

Let's connect: The Bible says that it's better to give than to receive. God blesses us when we give.

Initial discussion:
Which person did you choose, and why?

What do we learn about God in this book?

Sow and reap - 2 Corinthians 9: 6-7

To share our love, our work and even our money is a way of sowing. Just like if a farmer sows many seeds he will reap many fruits, also if we are willing to saw abundantly in people's lives, we will reap abundantly. The harvest will not be given to us by people, but by God.
That is what the apostle Paul wanted to teach the Corinthians, and he said: "Everyone has to determine how much he will give. Let us not give with sadness or because they we are obligated to give, because God loves the cheerful giver."

Question for us: In whom have you sown love, effort or money lately?

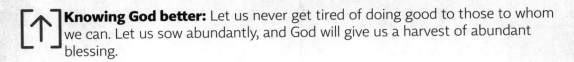

Knowing God better: Let us never get tired of doing good to those to whom we can. Let us sow abundantly, and God will give us a harvest of abundant blessing.

GOD REWARDS.

The weapons we can use to fight - 2 Corinthians 10: 4-5

Paul encourages us not to use the same ways of solving our problems that are used by people who do not know about God. Paul writes to the Corinthians saying: "To destroy the forces of evil, we do not use human weapons, but the weapons of God's power."

People who don't know about God want to solve things with certain weapons and forces, but we use other types of weapons. For example, prayer is a powerful weapon because we pray to a tremendously powerful God. Telling the truth is another powerful weapon powerful if we believe in God. The Bible is full of truths that help us fight against the arguments and lies of the world.

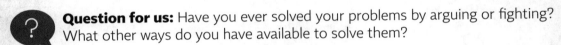

Question for us: Have you ever solved your problems by arguing or fighting? What other ways do you have available to solve them?

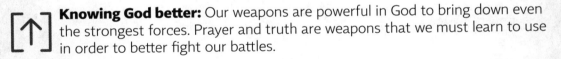

Knowing God better: Our weapons are powerful in God to bring down even the strongest forces. Prayer and truth are weapons that we must learn to use in order to better fight our battles.

GOD IS POWERFUL.

Main characters
Paul: apostle of Jesus who was entrusted to speak to non-Jews.
Corinthians: inhabitants of the region of Corinth.

Recommendation of verse to memorize:

2nd Corinthians 10:18

For it is not the one who commends himself who is approved, but the one whom the Lord commends.

What other verses would you add?

_____   _____
_____   _____
_____   _____

Download the "Family Readings and Conversations" from:
www.e625.com/lessons

Lesson 37 > ROMANS

General information about the book
Letter of the apostle Paul to the Romans; It addresses our Christian beliefs.
The letter has 16 chapters.

Who wrote it and in what era?
It was written by the apostle Paul, most likely in 56 A.D.

Purpose of the book
Paul wrote this letter to the Christians who lived in Rome, to remind them that the gospel offered salvation to both Jews and non-Jews.

Introductory activity
Checkers
We will play a checkers tournament. The rules are like this:
The checkers can only be moved forward diagonally on the dark squares, and can never move backward. When an opposing checker has an empty square behind it, it can be removed it by jumping over it.
A checker becomes a king when it reaches the last line of the opposing field. You "crown" it by placing another piece of the same color on top of it.
The king moves diagonally, but it can move forward or backward.

Let's connect: In games like this one or chess, the person who manages to see more than one move at a time and gets ahead of the play will win. God has control of our life, and although sometimes we do not understand his moves, He is in control and everything happens for our own good.

Initial discussion:
What was most difficult for you in the game?

What do we learn about God in this book?

Everything works together for good - Romans 8:28
Sometimes we don't understand why something we wanted very much doesn't work out the way we hoped for, or why sometimes things that appear to be bad happen to us. Paul tells the brothers from the church in Rome that all things work together for good for those who love the Lord.

Question for us: Do you remember something that seemed like a bad thing, that later ended up being a good thing?

 Knowing God better: We can trust that God has control of our lives and that He will make things work out for good.

GOD IS SOVEREIGN.

No one can separate us - Romans 8: 38-39

Imagine how powerful God's love is that nothing, absolutely nothing, can separate us from his love. There is no power, no creature, nothing in the highest, nothing in the deepest that can separate us from Jesus' love for us.

 Question for us: What do you think is the most powerful creature on earth?

 Knowing God better: No creature, however powerful, may separate us from the love of God.

GOD IS POWERFUL.

Do not conform to this world - Romans 12: 2

It is very easy for the fashions or thoughts of this world to influence us. Without realizing it, we act according to what we see on television or on the Internet. Paul asks the church not to get caught up in the fashions of this world.

 Question for us: What is your favorite program on TV or the internet?

 Knowing God better: Even though there are some good things in the programs we watch on TV or on our tablets, we must always be aware and always question if what they are saying is true or not, and if it is pleasing to God.

DIOS ES SANTO.

Main characters

Paul: apostle of Jesus who was entrusted to speak to non-Jews.
Romans: residents of the city of Rome.

Recommendation of verse to memorize:

Romans 8:31

What, then, shall we say in response to these things? If God is for us, who can be against us?

What other verses would you add?

_____   _____

_____   _____

_____   _____

Download the "Family Readings and Conversations" from:
www.e625.com/lessons

Lesson 38 > EPHESIANS

General information about the book
Letter from the apostle Paul to the Ephesians, explaining the blessing of the body of Christ.
The letter has 6 chapters.

Who wrote it and in what era?
It was written by the apostle Paul, most likely in the years 60 to 62 A.D.

Purpose of the book
Paul wrote Ephesians to teach us about the riches of God.

Introductory activity
We will need soft balls. We will divide into two teams: one team will throw the balls and the other team's members will have a shield (it can be made of cardboard) to defend themselves. If a ball hits a player, he must leave the game. If a thrower is touched by a person with a shield, he must exit the game. After five minutes, the team with the most players remaining wins.

Let's connect: Our fight is against those who want to get us to disobey God. We must be sure to always wear the right armor to withstand their attacks.

Initial discussion:
What do we need to be able to fight and defend ourselves if we are being attacked with darts?

What do we learn about God in this book?

Ephesians 6: 13-17
Paul encourages us to wear armor like the ones worn by the warriors of his era. This armor is figurative. He uses it to give us an example of how we should behave.

The belt of truth. The soldiers wore loose robes. The belt of truth represents the idea that we should not take the truth half-way, but should be fully confident in the truth of His word.
The breastplate of justice. The breastplate was made of sturdy leather that protected all the vital organs, like the heart.
The shield of faith refers to protection against darts, the thoughts that are not

of God.

The helmet of salvation. This refers to the fact that the devil wants to make us think that salvation is not valuable.

The sword of the Spirit, that is the Word. The sword is the attack weapon of the armor. When a thought comes to you, you must answer with the Word of God. That is why it is so important that we read the Bible.

Question for us: Which Bible verse would you choose to answer, if the following thoughts come to you?

You will not be able to do this.

Disobey your parents.

Take revenge for what they did to you.

Lying doesn't matter.

Knowing God better: God left us his Spirit and his Word to enable us to fight evil thoughts. When we feel attracted to do something wrong, let's protect ourselves with God's armor.

GOD PROTECTS US.

Ephesians 6: 1-3

The commandment to obey our parents is the first one that has a promise from God. God promises us that if we honor our parents we will do well and we will have a long life. Honoring them means making them proud of us, because we obey them and strive to do what's right.

Question for us: How do you think we can honor our parents?

Knowing God better: There are many ways to make our parents proud. Let us strive to honor them. God, who never lies, will give us His promise, and we will do well in life.

GOD IS OUR FATHER.

Main characters

Paul: apostle of Jesus who was entrusted to speak to non-Jews.

Ephesians: inhabitants of the region of Ephesus.

Recommendation of verse to memorize:

Ephesians 4:32

Be kind and compassionate to one another, forgiving each other, just as in Christ God forgave you.

What other verses would you add?

_____   _____
_____   _____
_____   _____

Download the "Family Readings and Conversations" from:
 www.e625.com/lessons

Lesson 39 > PHILIPPIANS

General information about the book
Letter from the apostle Paul to the Philippians. Describe Jesus as a source of joy and strength.
The letter has 4 chapters.

Who wrote it and in what era?
It was written by the apostle Paul, most likely in the year 61 A.D.

Purpose of the book
Paul wrote Philippians to teach us about the joy and the strength of God. This letter was written for those who lived in the region of Philippi.

Introductory activity
Get Serious. We will divide into pairs, and one person will be serious and not laugh, and the other person will do everything possible to make him laugh (without touching him). You can tell jokes, make faces, mimics, etc.

Let's connect: Did you know that when we laugh our body releases a substance that makes us feel good, and is good for our body? Laughing is healthy for our body.

Initial discussion:
Do you laugh often, or do you have a hard time laughing?

What do we learn about God in this book?

Pressing towards the goal - Philippians 3: 13-14

Paul compares our life in the Lord with a race. Has anyone ran a race? In a race the important thing is to reach the goal. If a person looks back, he will stop moving forward and will lose the race. In a race the important thing is consistency, always keeping the pace, and at the end make a last effort. You are just starting the race, so don't let anything distract you; Many things will try to separate you or distract you from the path, but you must remain strong and firm until you reach the goal. The goal is to become like Jesus.

Question for us: How many of you have run a race? What do you need to do to win a race?

Knowing God better: Just as you need training and discipline in order to win a race, the discipline of a Christian is to read the Bible, pray, and seek to do good to whoever we can.

GOD IS THE GOAL.

Do nothing out of selfishness - Philippians 2: 3

Paul said: "Do nothing out of selfishness or vanity. Rather, do everything humbly, considering others as better than yourself. " It really is very unpleasant when people are showing off their deeds, or do things just to be admired and to hear others say how good they are. When we do something for someone, we should not expect to be praised. Jesus said that if they praise us on earth, we've already had our reward, but if they don't, we will have our reward in heaven. Which reward do you prefer?

 Question for us: Have you ever done something for someone without expecting to be thanked?

 Knowing God better: Try to live without selfishness, and don't think only about winning for yourself. Be also happy when someone you love wins or does something well. Do not try to do things just to be admired.

GOD IS HUMBLE.

 Main characters
Paul: Apostle of Jesus who was entrusted to speak to non-Jews.
Philippians: inhabitants of the Philippi region.

 Recommendation of verse to memorize:
Philippians 2:5

Have the same mindset as Christ Jesus.

What other verses would you add?

_____   _____
_____   _____
_____   _____

 Download the "Family Readings and Conversations" from:
www.e625.com/lessons

Lesson 40> COLOSSIANS

General information about the book
Letter from the apostle Paul to the Colossians stressing that Jesus makes man perfect.
The letter has 4 chapters.

Who wrote it and in what era?
It was written by the apostle Paul, most likely between 60 and 62 A.D. Paul writes this letter from jail.

Purpose of the book
Paul wrote Colossians to teach us about the Son. This letter was written for those who lived in the Colosse region, a small village, and then it would be sent to the church of the great city of Laodicea.

Introductory activity
Positive attitude
We will separate into teams. Each team must agree so that one person comes forward and does something to make everybody laugh. The winner will be the team that does it with the best possible attitude, getting everybody to laugh

Let's connect: Paul motivates us to always live with a positive attitude, always doing things for the Lord and not for men.

Initial discussion:
What type of work that your parents or your teachers tell you to do is the most difficult one for you to do with a positive attitude?

What do we learn about God in this book?

The supremacy of Christ - Colossians 1: 15-20
Jesus is preeminent over all creation; Through Him all things were made. He is the head of the body that is the church. He is the firstborn in everything. Jesus is God. This is one of the clearest statements in the Bible about who Jesus is. Paul invites us to recognize Jesus as God and supreme. It highlights how, being so great, He loves us who are so small.

Question for us: What body function would you like to be?

 Knowing God better: Christ is the head and His church is His body. Just as in our body the head directs us and thinks, and the body acts according to those thoughts.

CHRIST IS THE FIRST.

Not with a bad attitude - Colossians 3:23

Paul told the Colossians: "Whatever you do, do it well, as if instead of working for earthly masters you were working for the Lord." Many times we do things that we may not like (but are good for us) with a bad attitude. For example, study; At times we may not do it willingly. The next time we have to do something that's good and we don't feel like doing it, let's think that we are doing it for The Lord, and He will rejoice with us.

 Question for us: What is the hardest thing for you to do, that don't do with a good attitude?

 Knowing God better: Exercising, studying, eating, helping with chores at home, are things that we have trouble doing with a good attitude. Let us understand that if we do things for the Lord, He will bless our lives because of our attitude.

GOD REWARDS.

 Main characters
Paul: apostle of Jesus who was entrusted to speak to non-Jews.
Colossians: inhabitants of the Colossi region.
Timothy: Paul's assistant.

 Recommendation of verse to memorize:
Colossians 3:20

Children, obey your parents in everything, for this pleases the Lord.

What other verses would you add?

_____   _____
_____   _____
_____   _____

 Download the "Family Readings and Conversations" from:
www.e625.com/lessons

Lesson 41 > PHILEMON

General information about the book
Letter from the apostle Paul to a believer named Philemon.
The letter has 1 chapter.

Who wrote it and in what era?
It was written by the apostle Paul, most likely between 60 and 62 A.D. Paul writes this letter to a man named Philemon, member of the congregation at Colossae.

Purpose of the book
Paul writes this letter to Philemon, a wealthy person, who had a slave named Onesimus, who had offended him. Paul asks Philemon to receive and forgive Onesimus.

Introductory activity
The weight of not forgiving
Let's keep our hands up for two minutes. Let's see who can keep them up.
Now let's put a weight like a book or anything light enough to be able to lift. We'll see for how long we can hold it.

Let's connect: How did you feel when the weight was removed? It felt good, right? This is how it feels when a person forgives. At first, not forgiving may seem bearable, but as time passes the load becomes heavier.

Initial discussion:
What would you think of someone who was forgiven a large debt, and then was unwilling to forgive someone who owed him very little?

What do we learn about God in this book?

Parable of the ruthless servant - Matthew 18: 21-25
Let's read this parable from the Gospel of Matthew about a person who owed a king a lot of money. The king had mercy on him and decided to forgive him the debt, because he knew it was impossible for him to pay it. Not even if he worked his whole life would he be able to afford it. Then, the person who was forgiven, found another person who owed him some money. What do you think was his reaction? The logical thing would have been to forgive him the little money he was owed, because he had been forgiven a lot. Well, he did not do so, and forced the person

who owed him little to pay him. When the king found out about it, he became very angry and sent him to jail. This same story happens to us when we don't forgive a person for an offense, because God has forgiven us for bigger offenses.

 Question for us: How many times should we forgive a person?

 Knowing God better: Jesus said that we should forgive up to seventy times seven, which means that we should always forgive.

GOD FORGIVES US.

Philemon - Philemon 1

We speak of forgiveness because it is the central theme of Philemon's letter. Philemon was a wealthy person who had a slave named Onesimus. Onesimus stole money from Philemon and went to Rome (That's what the slaves who stole used to do so they wouldn't get caught). While in Rome he met Paul and converted to Jesus. Onesimus served Paul and Paul loved him very much. Now Paul wanted Onesimus to return to Philemon, and he wanted Philemon to forgive him and no longer treat him as a slave but as a brother in Christ.

Paul's request to Philemon was difficult but Paul was sure that Philemon would forgive Onesimus because Christ had forgiven Philemon much more.

 Question for us: What are the things your friends do to you that are most difficult to forgive?

 Knowing God better: We can trust that forgiving others is always the best option, because God has forgiven us much more.

GOD HAS MERCY.

 Main characters
Paul: apostle of Jesus who was entrusted to speak to non-Jews.
Philemon: believer at the church of Colossae.
Onesimus: Philemon's slave who had fled and served Paul.

 Recommendation of verse to memorize:

Philemon 1: 3

Grace and peace to you from God our Father and the Lord Jesus Christ.

What other verses would you add?

—————————   ——————————————————————————————

—————————   ——————————————————————————————

—————————   ——————————————————————————————

 Download the "Family Readings and Conversations" from:
www.e625.com./lessons

Lesson 42> 1ST TIMOTHY, TITUS

General information about the book
These are letters from Pablo to his helpers, identified by their names.
1 Timothy has 6 chapters.
Titus has 3 chapters.

Who wrote it and in what era?
The apostle Paul wrote them most likely between A.D. 62 and 64. Paul writes his letter to his beloved disciple Timothy at Ephesus, and his letter to Titus on the island of Crete.

Purpose of the book
Paul wrote these letters to give instructions to his disciples, so they can teach them to the churches. The challenge was that they were young people trying to teach older people.

Introductory activity
Teaching origami
We will choose a group, and an adult will teach them to make a paper figure using origami. Then, each member of this group will have the responsibility of teaching it to another group. We will see how good we are as teachers.

Let's connect: Paul gave Timothy and Titus the mission of teaching the churches. Teaching is a difficult task, especially if you have to teach people who are older than you.

Initial discussion:
Did you ever have to teach something to someone older than you?

What do we learn about God in this book?

Be an example - 1st Timothy 4:12
Paul writes to Timothy, giving him instructions for the church, but asks him to set an example for others. He says: "Let no one despise you for being young. But be an example to the faithful in the way you speak and live, in love, in faith and in purity. "

We are very young, and we must be an example for others. If we say that we must behave well, we must also do it, because others will believe us more if they see that we do than based on what we say.
Paul asks the same of Titus in Titus 2: 7.

 Question for us: When have you behaved as an example for others?

 Knowing God better: Although we may not always be able to behave as well as we should, we must always try, because there are many people watching us and learning from us. We were called to be a light to the world.

GOD SEES US.

Physical exercise - 1st Timothy 4: 8

Is physical exercise good for us? Of course. To grow up healthy and strong, we need to exercise daily. Paul tells Timothy that exercise is good but that, just as he should do physical exercises, he should also exercised his piety towards others.

When we exercise, we start with small, simple exercises until we can do more difficult and complete exercises. Let's start by doing small works of piety, and keep exercising our piety until we become like Jesus.

 Question for us: What small exercise in piety can you do this week?

 Knowing God better: Helping others, sharing your food, teaching someone something they don't know, these are all small exercises in piety that we should practice.

GOD IS LOVE.

 Main characters
Paul: apostle of Jesus who was entrusted to speak to non-Jews.
Titus: disciple of Paul.
Timothy: disciple of Paul, son of Eunice and Grandson of Loida.

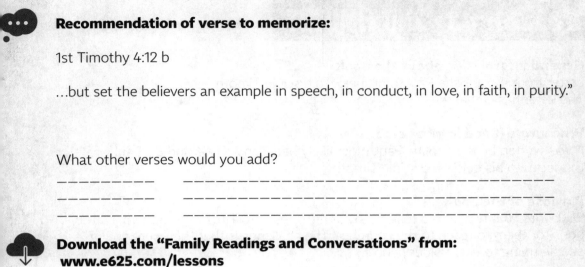

Recommendation of verse to memorize:

1st Timothy 4:12 b

...but set the believers an example in speech, in conduct, in love, in faith, in purity."

What other verses would you add?

_____   _____
_____   _____
_____   _____

Download the "Family Readings and Conversations" from:
www.e625.com/lessons

Lesson 43 > 2ND TIMOTHY

General information about the book
Letter from the apostle Paul to his beloved disciple Timothy.
The letter has 4 chapters.

Who wrote it and in what era?
It was written by the apostle Paul, most likely between A.D. 66 and 68. Paul wrote this letter to his beloved disciple Timothy.

Purpose of the book
Paul writes the two letters to Timothy and the letter to Titus to give them instructions for them to teach to the churches. The challenge is that they were young people trying to teach older people.

Introductory activity
Soldiers of Jesus
We will stand in formation as soldiers in a line. An adult should give instructions such as "lie on the ground," "take a step to the right," "take a step to the left," "jump twice," etc. Whoever makes a mistake must leave the competition.

Let's connect: We are our Lord's soldiers. A soldier needs lots of training, and must follow the orders of his superior. Our superior is God and our training is prayer, bible reading, and good deeds.

Initial discussion:
How do you imagine a soldier's training?

What do we learn about God in this book?

Spirit of power - 2nd Timothy 1: 6-7
Paul was in jail for the second time, and most people had left him alone. He writes this second letter to his dear disciple Timothy to ask him to visit him. Even though Paul was imprisoned and in a very difficult situation, he tells Timothy that he should not be ashamed or intimidated, because the Gospel is the power of God. God has not given us a Spirit of fear, but a Spirit of power, love and self-control.

Question for us: Have you ever been ashamed of saying that you are a Christian, or of preaching about Jesus?

 Knowing God better: Even if our friends make fun of us for being followers of Jesus, we should know that the Gospel is the power of God and that God is pleased when we talk about Him with others.

GOD CALLS US TO BE HIS WITNESSES.

Good testimony - 2nd Timothy 2:15

To give testimony of Jesus before others is to not be ashamed of being followers and believers in Him, and to do what his word tells us to do. Paul encourages Timothy to strive to present himself as a worker acceptable unto God, since it requires an effort to be able to do what Jesus has told us to do.

When we fail an exam, we have to try harder and take it again until we pass it. Likewise, if we fail and do something wrong before God, God will forgive us if we ask Him for it, and we will have to work harder to pass that exam.

 Question for us: Have you ever failed an exam? What did you have to do to pass it?

 Knowing God better: Hard work always brings rewards. Striving to be acceptable unto God is worthwhile, and it brings benefits and rewards.

GOD GIVES SECOND CHANCES.

 Main characters
Paul: apostle of Jesus who was entrusted to speak to non-Jews.
Timothy: disciple of Paul, son of Eunice and Grandson of Loida.

 Recommendation of verse to memorize:

2nd Timothy 1:7

For the Spirit God gave us does not make us timid, but gives us power, love and self-discipline.

What other verses would you add?

_____   _____

_____   _____

_____   _____

 Download the "Family Readings and Conversations" from:
 www.e625.com/lessons

Lesson 44> 1ST PETER

General information about the book
First letter of the apostle Peter, sent to believers who had been expelled from their land and were going through a crisis.
The letter has 5 chapters.

Who wrote it and in what era?
It was written by the apostle Peter, most likely between AD 64 and 65.

Purpose of the book
Peter was in jail when he wrote this letter, and he encourages believers to trust God. In the midst of affliction there is always hope in Him!

Introductory activity
Living rocks
Let's make human pyramids. With great care we will make a pyramid putting several kids as a base. When finished, be ready for someone to take a picture of the final result.

Let's connect:
Peter says that we are living rocks that form a spiritual house.

Initial discussion:
What part of the house do you like best?

What do we learn about God in this book?

Be holy - 1st Peter 1: 14-15

Peter encourages us to be obedient children, and to not conform to this world. What does it mean to not conform to this world? It means not to do the evil things that people do. To conform to this world is, for example, to isolate a child from your class and not talk to him anymore. We would conform to this world if we did things just because others do them. When something is wrong and we do it, we conform to this world.

Question for us: What example can you come up with of conforming to this world?

Knowing God better: To conform means to take the form. We must be strong and resist doing evil when we know we must do good.

GOD IS HOLY.

Do not be ashamed - 1st Peter 4:14

Peter said: "If you are insulted because of the name of Christ, you are blessed, for the Spirit of glory and of God rests on you." Sometimes there are people who can make fun of us for saying that we are Christians or for doing what Jesus told us to do. If someone does this to us, the apostle Peter encouraged us not to be ashamed but to praise God because God rejoices with us.

 Question for us: What would you answer if someone made fun of you for being a Christian?

 Knowing God better: Jesus rejoices every time we talk about him with our friends.

GOD REJOICES WITH US WHEN WE TALK ABOUT HIM.

 Main characters
Peter: apostle of Jesus who was entrusted to speak to the Jews.

Recommendation of verse to memorize:

1st Peter 4:8

Above all, love each other deeply, because love covers over a multitude of sins.

What other verses would you add?

_____   _____
_____   _____
_____   _____

 Download the "Family Readings and Conversations" from:
www.e625.com/lessons

Lesson 45 > 2ND PETER

General information about the book
Second letter of the apostle Peter, written to alert Christians about the lies that were spreading and opposing the truth of God.
The letter has 3 chapters.

Who wrote it and in what era?
It was written by the apostle Peter, most likely between AD 64 and 65. Peter was in jail when he wrote this letter to encourage believers to trust God.

Purpose of the book
Peter knew he was near death. He wanted to warn believers about the lies they were listening to and he wanted them to be clear about the teachings regarding the return of Christ and the end of the world.

Introductory activity
Two truths and a lie
To play "two truths and a lie" everyone sits in a circle. Each participant prepares three statements, two that are true and one that is a lie. The order of the participants is chosen at random to share their three statements. According to the rules, the objective is to decide which of the three statements is a lie. An example: "I have two sisters, my middle name is Alberto and I study karate." The more people in the room know about you, the more difficult the game becomes.

Let's connect: Peter was very concerned because there were many false prophets looking to teach lies to the church.

Initial discussion:
Do you remember any lie that you believed?

What do we learn about God in this book?

Remember scriptures - 2 Peter 1:12
Peter insists that the church should always study the truth, and says the following: "I will always remind you of these things, even though you know them and are firmly established in the truth you now have."

Sometimes we might say that we already know a Bible story, or that it is not necessary to memorize texts. Peter said it was necessary to be reminded of it, no matter how much we already know it, to ensure that no one will be able to teach us anything that is not written in the Bible. Many false prophets have wanted to teach the church things that are wrong, and Peter knew that the only way we could reject their teachings was for us to know the truth, and that's why he insisted on reminding us.

 Question for us: What verse or passage from the Bible do you know?

 Knowing God better: The apostle Peter asks us to insist in learning and knowing the Bible, so that no one can deceive us by teaching us things that are not of God, even within the Church.

GOD IS UNIQUE.

From faith to love - 2 Peter 1: 5-8

According to Peter, the qualities that will make us grow in the knowledge of Jesus are:
Faith
Good behavior
Understanding
Self-control
Patience
Devotion to God
Fraternal affection
Love

It looks like the apostle Peter placed these characteristics in order, and said to add love to all of them. Paul also said in the letter to the Corinthians that of all characteristics the most important one is love.

 Question for us: Can we each give an example of some of the characteristics that Peter spoke of in 2 Peter 1: 5-7?

 Knowing God better: To grow in the knowledge of Jesus will take us our whole lifetime, but we must be clear that what's important about growing in knowledge is to do it with love and not with arrogance.

GOD REJOICES WITH US WHEN WE TALK ABOUT HIM.

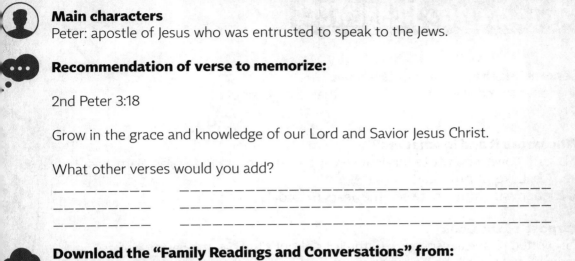

Main characters

Peter: apostle of Jesus who was entrusted to speak to the Jews.

Recommendation of verse to memorize:

2nd Peter 3:18

Grow in the grace and knowledge of our Lord and Savior Jesus Christ.

What other verses would you add?

_____   _____
_____   _____
_____   _____

Download the "Family Readings and Conversations" from:
www.e625.com/lessons

Lesson 46 › HEBREWS

General information about the book
The letter to the Hebrews emphasizes that Jesus is simply better.
It has 13 chapters.

Who wrote it and in what era?
It is not known who wrote this letter. Possible authors are Paul, Silas, Barnabas, Apollos, Luke, or others.
The letter was written between the years 67 and 69 A.D.

Purpose of the book
It is written to speak especially to the Jews about Christ as the Savior, and as the one who fulfilled all the promises about the Savior foretold in the Old Testament.

Introductory activity
Who is it?
We will divide into two teams: one will ask questions and another one will only be allowed to answer yes or no. On the foreheads of those who ask questions we will put names of the heroes of the faith. Their task will be to try to find out the names on their forehead with their questions. They cannot ask about letters.

Let's connect: The letter to the Hebrews describes many heroes of the faith. They are characters who believed and had hope.

Initial discussion:
Do any of you have the name of a Bible character?

What do we learn about God in this book?

Heroes of faith - Hebrews 11
The letter to the Hebrews defines faith as the reality of what is hoped for, the assurance of what is not seen.

In the Old Testament there are many examples of men of faith: Abel, Enoch, Noah, Abraham, Isaac, Jacob, Joseph, Moses, Rahab, Gideon and several others. Many of these were men with defects and virtues, but they all had faith.

They were certain that God was with them, but none of them knew Jesus. We have the privilege of being able to have faith and also knowing that Jesus is the Son of God.

Question for us: Who is the hero of faith whose story you like best?

Knowing God better: Faith is the assurance that what we hope for will happen. Our faith must always be placed in God.

GOD IS MY ASSURANCE.

Jesus, High Priest - Hebrews 4: 12-16, 11, 12: 1-4

The letter to the Hebrews was written to help Christians who were Jews. It says: "The word of God is alive and powerful. It is sharper than a two-edged sword that penetrates to the deepest part of our being, and examines our innermost thoughts and desires of our heart."

It helps us evaluate what is good and what is bad. Thanks to that we cannot hide anything before God, but we must not be afraid. We have a High Priest, Jesus, who understands our weaknesses as a human, because He lived as a man and suffered just like us, but did not sin.

Question for us: What do you think are things that Jesus experienced as a human?

Knowing God better: Jesus got tired, hungry, and sleepy. He had pain, he cried and he laughed. Jesus understands what we go through because He experienced it on earth.

JESUS IS OUR HIGH PRIEST.

Main characters
The heroes of faith: Abel, Enoch, Abraham, Isaac, Jacob, Joseph, among others.

Recommendation of verse to memorize:

Hebrews 13:8

Jesus Christ the same yesterday, and today, and forever.

What other verses would you add?

_____   _____

_____   _____

_____   _____

 Download the "Family Readings and Conversations" from:
www.e625.com/lessons

Lesson 47 > 1ST, 2ND AND 3RD JOHN

General information about the book
The letters of the apostle John were very important to explain that Jesus is truly God and truly man, and how we should live as his disciples.
The first letter has five chapters, the second and third have one chapter each.

Who wrote it and in what era?
These letters were written by the apostle John between the years 90 to 95 A.D. John was the last apostle to die.

Purpose of the books
John emphasizes that we should love one another as brothers to show that God's love dwells in us, and also as evidence that we love God.

Introductory activity
Love the one who needs it
We will put stickers on our foreheads with words like "sick", "poor", "deaf" and others that come to mind. We will all act with love towards others by providing them help, according to the sticker they are wearing. No one can see their own sticker and in the end everyone will have to guess, according to the type of help they received, which one they had on their own foreheads.

Let's connect: The main message of John's letters is that we should show love to our brethren.

Initial discussion:
How did you feel about the way you were treated?

What do we learn about God in this book?

Loving with actions - 1 John 3: 16-18
John speaks of a new commandment, to love our brethren with a love like Jesus' love for us. When John says to give our lives for our brother, he does not necessarily mean that we should die for them. He is telling us to help our brothers with whatever means we have at our disposal. If anyone asks for help, help him. This is to demonstrate with actions God's love for him. John said: "If anyone has mate-

rial possessions and sees a brother or sister in need but has no pity on them, how can the love of God be in that person? Dear children, let us not love with words or speech but with actions and in truth. "

 Question for us: How do you think you can demonstrate God's love to your friends?

 Knowing God better: God's love must be demonstrated with actions, not only with words. God is love, and that is why we love, because we are from God.

DIOS ES AMOR.

Loving my brother - 1 John 4:21

I cannot say that I love God if I am quarreling with my brothers or with my friends. John tells us that we cannot say that we love God, whom we do not see, if we do not love our brothers whom we see.

The next time you fight with someone, remember that God does not like that attitude because, by fighting with someone whom God loves, you are not showing that you love Him.

 Question for us: Have you ever quarreled with someone you love?

 Knowing God better: God's love is shown by forgiving, not by quarreling.

JESUS FORGIVES US, THAT'S WHY WE FORGIVE.

 Main characters
John: apostle loved by Jesus.

 Recommendation of verse to memorize:

1st John 3:16

This is how we know what love is: Jesus Christ laid down his life for us. And we ought to lay down our lives for our brothers and sisters.

What other verses would you add?

_____   _____
_____   _____
_____   _____

Download the "Family Readings and Conversations" from:
www.e625.com/lessons

Lesson 48 › JUDE

General information about the book
It is one of the general letters of the New Testament.
It has only 1 chapter.

Who wrote it and in what era?
It is written by Jude, brother of James. If so, then he is also a brother of Jesus. However, very little is known of his life. He writes it around the year 60 A.D.

Purpose of the book
Judas had planned to write a letter to believers to talk about the subject of salvation. However, he realized that people were affecting the church by telling lies about Jesus, so he decided to change the subject. He wrote to them about how they must defend Jesus' truths not only with words, but mainly through a life of obedience.

Introductory activity
We are going to review some television programs, series or cartoons that most of us have seen. As we know, on television or in videos, it is possible to use many special effects. Some things are exaggerations, others are impossible in the real world. Let's see if we can make a list of the biggest lies we've seen.

Let's connect: In videos or movies we can detect the lies. However, imagine for a moment what would happen if someone did not realize that something was not true, and believed that it was true. It would be disastrous! He could get seriously injured.

Initial discussion:
Do you think that everyone knows the truth about God? What would happen if someone does not know the truth, or believes lies about God?

What do we learn about God in this book?

Jude 1: 3-4
The Christians to whom Judas writes had been infiltrated by people who spoke lies about Jesus. Unfortunately those Christians had done nothing about it; they lis-

tened, and even began to believe some of these lies! Judas reminds them that those who have believed the true gospel show it in their lives of obedience. Those who speak a false gospel demonstrate it with a life of disobedience.

 Question for us: Why do you think it is that the way we live gives away what we believe about Jesus?

 Knowing God better: When we know Jesus, our life is transformed from within. The Bible says that we are made new people (new creatures) and then people begin to be noticed our way of life, in obedience to God.

GOD TRANSFORMS US.

Jude 1: 12-13, 16

Judas warns Christians that liars are saying that it's possible to obey God and keep sinning. This is false. So, he describes those who teach lies in four ways. Think for a moment about the meaning of each of these descriptions. Now think about the opposite of these descriptions, about a person who knows, speaks and lives the truths of the Word of God.

 Question for us: Which of these descriptions gets your attention the most?

 Knowing God better: In Jesus we know the generous, loving, helpful and humble character of God. He expects us, his children, to reflect these same attributes towards others, because we know Him.

GOD IS NOT SELFISH.

(Judas 1: 20-22)

Amidst the lies that some were teaching, Judas asks believers for two important things. First, he tells them that they must stay firm in knowing and believing only the truth. In other words, they must be alert in order to not be fooled! Second, he asks them to please try to help others to not believe the lies, and to rescue them from committing disastrous mistakes. When we know the truth we must teach it to others.

Question for us: Who can you talk to about Jesus this week?

Knowing God better: God is merciful and always wants us to know him. He doesn't want us to be deceived by false gods, or false ideas about what pleases Him. The only way to know the truth is is to read his Word and obey it.

GOD IS TRUTH.

Main characters
Jude: church leader, brother of Jesus.

Recommendation of verse to memorize:

Jude 1: 3b

Contend for the faith that was once for all entrusted to God's holy people.

What other verses would you add?

_____   _____
_____   _____
_____   _____

**Download the "Family Readings and Conversations" from:
www.e625.com/lessons**

Lesson 49 > REVELATION (part one)

Chapters 1 to 5

General information about the book

Book written by the apostle John; it's the last book of the Bible, and it contains many messages about the future.
It has 22 chapters.

Who wrote it and in what era?

It was written by the apostle John between the years 94 and 96 A.D.

Purpose of the book

John is led to have a vision in which he sees what was happening in heaven; This is what he presents in this book. He describes heaven and future events at the time of the second coming of the Lord Jesus.

Introductory activity:

Heavenly praise
We will divide into four groups:

    Lions
    Bulls
    Humans
    Eagles

Each group will try to imagine what it will be like to sing the song "Hallelujah" as each of the mentioned figures. Once we are in agreement, we will all sing the song for God.

Let's connect: The apostle John saw what worship in heaven was like. One of the things he saw were four living beings that had these forms. Worship in heaven will be very creative!

Initial discussion:
How do you imagine worship in heaven?

What do we learn about God in this book?

The worship in heaven - Revelation 4

Have you ever imagined what worship in heaven will be like? John was taken there in a vision and was able to contemplate part of what a worship service in heaven

167

was like. What he saw was impressive. The first thing he saw was a throne that was surrounded by twenty-four thrones where twenty-four elders sat with gold crowns on their heads. He also saw a sea of glass! Around the throne he saw four living beings with different shapes. And all said: "Holy, Holy, Holy is the Lord God almighty, who was, who is and who is to come." Each time they worshiped, the twenty-four elders cast their crowns before the throne.

Anyway, the image was impressive.
Sometimes we don't give importance to worshipping God, and in heaven it will be something very important and creative!

 Question for us: What would you say to Jesus when you worship him in heaven?

 Knowing God better: Anything that you can think of telling Jesus when you get to heaven, you can tell Him today, and create the best worship. The best worship is the one that is genuine from your heart.

GOD IS MAJESTIC.

Correcting the churches - Revelation 1, 2 and 3

John was given a message for the churches. The message was about what they were doing right, but also what they were doing wrong. The Lord told John that he scolded them because he loved them. It is like our parents. They scold us because they love us. They also tell us good things, because they love us.
One of the things John was told was that God knocked on the door of our hearts and that it was our decision to receive Him and ask Him to enter. If we do not ask Him to enter, He will not. He loves us but He wants us to ask him to enter into our hearts.

 Question for us: Who wants to receive Jesus as the Lord of his life and to invite him to enter into his heart?

 Knowing God better: The Lord is knocking at the door of your heart. Open the door and invite Him to come in, so that He will live forever in your heart, to be your Lord!

JESUS IS A GENTLEMAN AND RESPECTFUL.

Main characters
John: apostle loved by Jesus.

Recommendation of verse to memorize:

Revelation 3:19

Those whom I love I rebuke and discipline.

What other verses would you add?

_____   _____
_____   _____
_____   _____

Download the "Family Readings and Conversations" from:
www.e625.com/lessons

Lesson 50 > REVELATION (part two)

Chapters 6 to 22

General information about the book
Book written by the apostle John; it's the last book of the Bible, and it contains many messages about the future.
It has 22 chapters.

Who wrote it and in what era?
It was written by the apostle John between the years 94 and 96 A.D.

Purpose of the book
John is led to have a vision in which he sees what was happening in heaven; This is what he presents in this book. He describes heaven and future events at the time of the second coming of the Lord Jesus.

Introductory activity
Heavenly construction
Using Legos, modeling clay or cardboard, we will build a city. In the city there must be a temple, there must be streets, a river, houses and many people worshiping. We will divide the work among all of us, and once we are done we will take a picture to remember our creation.

Let's connect: The apostle John saw that in heaven there is a new city, a new earth and new heavens. It will be very, very beautiful.

Initial discussion:
How do you imagine the heavenly city?

What do we learn about God in this book?

The New Jerusalem - Revelation 21

John described what he saw as new. He said: "Then I saw a new heaven and a new earth, because the earth, the sea and the sky we know were gone. And I saw the holy city, the new Jerusalem, descend from heaven, from where God was. It had the glorious and beautiful appearance of a bride."

He says that this new city was beautiful, it had lots of gold. There was no temple because the Lord was the temple. There was neither sun nor moon, because the Lord was the light. It was beautiful, very beautiful.

 Question for us: How do you want your house in heaven to be?

 Knowing God better: The Lord went to prepare houses for us, and from what John saw, everything will be very beautiful. Meanwhile, let us live our lives for Jesus, and when we get old and go to heaven, we will be able to enjoy the house that Jesus went to prepare for us.

GOD IS AWESOME.

The last battle - Revelation 19

After a great battle against the devil, the Lord was victorious and came back again through the heavens on a white horse. The eyes of the rider were like fire flames, and a sharp sword was coming out of his mouth.
The battle was impressive and Jesus came out as the victor. We serve a powerful God who will return for us, and his kingdom will have no end.

 Question for us: How do you imagine the return of Jesus through the heavens?

 Knowing God better: The Lord has promised to return, and we will be here waiting for Him with eager hearts and love for one another. Jesus is the same yesterday, today and forever!

JESUS WILL RETURN.

 Main characters
John: apostle loved by Jesus.
Jesus: will return for his people.

 Recommendation of verse to memorize:

Revelation 22:13

I am the Alpha and the Omega, the First and the Last, the Beginning and the End.

What other verses would you add?

_____   _____

_____   _____

_____   _____

Download the "Family Readings and Conversations" from:
www.e625.com/lessons

NOTES

NOTES

NOTES

NOTES

NOTES

NOTES

NOTES

NOTES

NOTES

NOTES

NOTES

NOTES

NOTES

NOTES

NOTES

SOME QUESTIONS TO ANSWER:

WHO IS BEHIND THIS BOOK?

E625 is a team of pastors and servants from different countries, different denominations, different sizes and church styles who love Christ and the new generations.

e625.com

WHAT IS E625.COM ABOUT?

Our passion is to help families and churches to find good materials and resources for the discipleship of new generations and that is why our website serves parents, pastors, teachers, and leaders 365 days a year through **www.e625.com** with free resources.

zona de contenido
PREMIUM

WHAT IS THE PREMIUM SERVICE?

In addition to free reflections and short materials, we have a service of lessons, series, research, online books, and audiovisual resources to facilitate your task. Your church can access them with a monthly subscription that allows all the leaders of a local church to share them as a team and make the necessary copies that they find pertinent to the different activities of the congregation or its families.

CAN I EQUIP MYSELF WITH YOU?

It would be a privilege to help you and with that objective, you can choose seminars at **www.e625.com** and academic courses at **www.institutoE625.com**.

Sign up for e625.com updates right now depending on your work arena: Pastors - Children - Preadolescents - Adolescents - College ministry.

LET'S LEARN TOGETHER!

e625.com

🅕 🅧 🅞 ▶/**e625**COM

Magazine

Books

Chat

Downloads
Subscription

Store

Events

Seminars

INSTITUTO
e6
25

Online Education
www.InstitutoE625.com

e625.com